The
Tattered
Passport

DAVID SNELL

DAVID SNELL

ISBN: 9781720238171

Dedication

To all the saints around the world who are working so diligently to make decent housing a reality for all of God's people and who so graciously invited me in. And to Sheilla, who always made me grateful to be home again.

Table of Contents

INTRODUCTION

BY CHRIS JOHNSON

Before I began working as Director of Communications for The Fuller Center for Housing in 2011, my international adventures consisted of a few hours in Windsor, Ontario, while attending a newspaper conference across the river in Detroit. At the time it seemed rather eventful going through a tunnel under a river to get to another country and then barely catching the last bus back home.

Then I met David Snell, the President of The Fuller Center for Housing. Having been a leader in the affordable housing movement since the early 1990s when he connected with Millard Fuller, David has seen the world in ways few others do — off the beaten path in many different countries.

Sure, he has been to well-known places like Paris but not to view the Eiffel Tower. No, it was just a stop on his way to the heart of the jungle in the Congo. Yes, he has traversed the busy streets of Beijing but only because he was jumping through hoops to get into North Korea ... more than once. He's the only person I know personally who has been to North Korea more than Dennis Rodman.

He has visited exotic places like Nepal and gotten to know the people of the sandy valleys well outside bustling Kathmandu. He has flown into busy Lima, Peru, and then taken buses to work in the arid highlands where families make lives from seemingly nothing. In places like El Salvador — a land often portrayed as gang-ridden and desperate — he has found families full of joy and hope.

Along the way, David kept journals about his experiences. Perhaps he did so just to occupy the many long hours he has spent waiting in airports for delayed flights and waiting in hotels for late rides. He writes about the strange foods — good, bad and occasionally disturbing — that have been placed before him. He notes the wide range of accommodations from unexpected luxuries to third-world starkness. And he details the transportation modes few have experienced, including pirogues in the jungles and hand-me-down Soviet aircraft.

However, just as The Fuller Center for Housing's work is ultimately about the people living in homes instead of the structures themselves, David's writings are about the people who make this world so fascinating. Some of them are movers and shakers, but most of them are just interesting characters, including those who, unlike David, have never even seen the world outside of their little villages.

When David first told me about his journals, I thought it was a little selfish for the guy to keep those stories all to himself. Thanks to today's ease of publishing, I won't let him keep them to himself any longer. We are sharing these journals "semi-edited." This is not a novel but more of a stream-of-consciousness reflection about the world as David was seeing it at the time. The only things added for this publication were short epilogues he provided about the current state of our work in each nation. Some of those are a rousing success, such as in Armenia and El Salvador, while others like North Korea turned out to be … well … learning opportunities.

What folks take from these writings will likely vary wildly. For me, as someone whose international travel experiences have broadened only slightly to include adventuresome travel in places like Ghana and Nicaragua with this work, my takeaway from so many of these stories is: "I'm glad you had this crazy adventure — and not me." Others will be envious — assuming those people always wondered what it would be like to be given the gift of a live chicken in Africa or to have to figure out what you would do if the airline for whom you had your connecting ticket would not come through because they crashed the only plane they had remaining in their lineup.

For those many intrepid volunteers who have worked with The Fuller Center's Global Builders program in Central and South America, Asia and Africa, some of these adventures will bring to mind their own experiences in such places. Seeing the world off the well-trodden tourist paths is quite the challenge but brings the most memorable experiences. I've met a lot of these folks, and I think some have practically become addicted to the thrills of circling this amazing planet.

To David Snell and the world travelers out there, I say more power to you! Few things enhance your perspective on life more than seeing the world beyond our borders. You are to be thanked for your service and lauded for your persistence and the number-one requirement for such global experiences — patience.

Still, David and most of those folks share one opinion that I've had for a long time — a view that has only grown more steadfast as I've edited these journal entries from a screened-in back porch here in Georgia (the state, not the country):

THE TATTERED PASSPORT

There's no place like home.

FOREWARD

In 1989 my wife Sheilla and I moved to Tijuana on what we thought was a six-month lark. Habitat for Humanity was planning the 1990 Jimmy Carter Work Project there and they needed a hand, specifically one that came attached to a Spanish speaker. We didn't realize that that short assignment would change our lives, and we've been involved in building houses for God's people in need ever since.

From Tijuana we ended up in Americus, Georgia, after another Jimmy Carter Work Project stint in Washington and Baltimore. We left Americus in 1997. Things were starting to change and being a good old traditionalist I thought it was time to move on. We thought that we'd finally made it home and settled back in Colorado.

In 2004 there was thunder coming from the east as long-simmering conflicts between Millard and the Habitat board were heating up. I figured that I could turn the tide of history so I waded right in, trying to find a way for Habitat to retain what I thought was its greatest asset—Millard Fuller. Didn't work. In December of 2004 Millard and Linda were fired from the organization that they founded and nurtured into the world's premier affordable housing ministry.

After the initial shock we started to look into what was next. Millard was not one to wallow and he said that he'd read the Bible backward and forward and couldn't find the work 'retirement' anywhere in it. So we put our heads together and formed what became The Fuller Center for Housing. We didn't intend for it to be a house builder, rather it was a platform for Millard to continue to do what he did best, preach and teach and motivate on behalf of the Habitat affiliates that he had tremendous affection for.

Two things happened in the fall of 2005 that forever changed our course. Hurricane Katrina hit and friends from Shreveport came over asking for help to house the thousands of people who had fled New Orleans and didn't want to go back. The second was a visit from a new friend who told us about a need and a solution in Nepal—you'll read more about that soon.

When word got out that Millard was building houses again the flood gates opened. We had people calling in from across the country and around the world asking to be a part of this new movement. I took on the assignment of Vice

President of Programs and thus began the greatest adventure that a guy with wanderlust could hope to have. Someone had to visit these potential build sites and that someone was me. I feel incredibly blessed to have been able to see the world as few others have.

Millard died in 2009 and his passing gave us pause. We wondered if we should or even could continue this work. But we had promises to keep and decided to forge ahead. I was asked to step in as president—a daunting assignment for sure. Millard's shoes were too large for any single pair of feet, but many feet have come together and the work goes on. But my travels have been curtailed. Ryan Iafigliola took on the assignment of Director of International Field Operations and he's now getting to see the world as I've seen it. There are many places that you'll read about here that I hope to return to someday but if I don't, what a storehouse of memories I've been able to collect. I'm honored to share some of them with you.

DAVID SNELL

NEPAL

THE TATTERED PASSPORT

I've been fascinated by the Himalayan countries for as long as I can remember. The first school report I recall writing was about Tibet and I believed everything that Lobsang Rampa wrote. If I'd known back then what a bucket list was, travel to that part of the world would have been on it. Little did I know when we were putting The Fuller Center together that that dream would come true.

In 2005 we were just getting underway when a man named Roscoe Douglas came to see Millard. He had just returned from Nepal and brought news of a gentleman there, a Mr. BL Shrestha, who had developed a simple solution to a serious problem in an area called the Terai, on the southern border with India. When we think of Nepal we generally have images of the towering Himalayas, which is accurate but incomplete. A short 150 miles south of Mt. Everest is the Terai, which sits at about 800 feet above sea level. The climate there is tropical with two seasons, rainy and dry. During the dry season hundreds of straw houses go up in flames so Mr. Shrestha, an engineer, developed a simple building system using woven mats covered with a concrete stucco to help minimize the fire risk. Amazingly, the simple house he designed could be built for $750. I told Millard, half tongue-in-cheek, that this would require a site visit, and son of a gun he agreed! So in September of 2005 I was off to tidy up the bucket list. Here are some of my notes about my time there.

From the moment the plane touches down in Kathmandu you know that you're in a mystical place. The area between the runways is filled with a type of pampa grass that waves gently as the plane goes by. In the distance you can see the top of the Boudhanath Stupa, one of the largest Buddhist temples in the world. Enchantment awaits.

It was a great trip—nice people, amazing sights, tolerable food—all told an amazing place. I'm so grateful to have been able to make the trip. If I never leave home again I will always have the memory of my time in Nepal. I'm not sure I can easily explain in words what I've seen. This is an ancient place. I visited temples that are 800 years old and still in active use.

You can't really talk about Nepal without talking about religion—it's a country of temples and shrines, many of them hundreds of years old. It is a deeply religious place, at least in terms of sites and ceremonies. It's harder to tell how religious it is in terms of faith, at least as we see it in the West. Both Hinduism and Buddhism teach morality but they don't have Sunday school or church services in the Western sense, so it's hard to tell what they teach and when they teach it.

Hinduism is the state religion and Buddhism is considered a traditional religion. Both were protected by the constitution of that time and proselytizing by any other religions was prohibited. Nonetheless there were an estimated 200,000 practicing Christians in the country at that time and my new friends were mightily engaged in the faith. Samuel Tamang, the man who agreed to take the leadership of our work there, is among them, busily planting churches all across the country when he wasn't teaching at the university or at his architecture practice.

We went to his church, Bethel Assembly of God, on Saturday—church day in Nepal. It was a new experience in the diversity that is Christianity. There are no pews in the chapel. The floors are covered with plush carpets and the men sat on one side and the women on the other. Everything was done in Nepali, so I missed the finer points of the sermon. There were a couple of solid, old hymns that I was able to sing along with. After the service we all retired to the courtyard for tea. My harshest memory of the day was when I was graciously offered a cup of tea which I accepted graciously and scalded my hand. I should have noticed that the tea was served in an aluminum glass. The more experienced congregants held them top to bottom between their thumb and middle finger.

During my time here they've had Fathers' Day, when people buy sweets for their fathers and pray for the departed. We also had Mothers' day and Women's day (although that could just be an extension of Mothers' day—hard to tell). On Mothers'/Women's Day all of the ladies dressed in red saris and danced in the streets, turning a 20-minute ride to the airport into a 50-minute event, with all of the detours around dancing, red-clad women.

The Hindu caste system, while constitutionally banned, seems to be alive and well. Everyone I spent any time with managed to subtly identify their caste and how it related to the others. This was true of Christians as well as Hindus. Apparently the Brahmin caste is reserved for priests. The next caste down is the warrior class, which is the caste of the king as well as the Shrestha's and the Chettis. Most everyone I met found a way to let me know that they were of the warrior class. Except for the Tamangs, who are ethnically Buddhist and are outside of the caste system. That means that they are just barely above the Scheduled Caste—the untouchables—as, apparently, am I.

We stayed at the Hyatt Regency and that's where we had most of our meetings. It was a little embarrassing to be talking with the local folks about poverty housing at one of Kathmandu's poshest hotels. I didn't make the arrangements so I could pass off the blame. One nice feature of the stay—the hotel is within walking distance of the Boudhanath Stupa so I was able to visit it. There are a good number of Tibetans in Nepal—refugees of the tragic Chinese occupation—and many of them live near the Stupa, so I was able to experience Tibet from afar.

We flew down to Janakpur, the capital of the area where we planned to build. We weren't able to visit the actual building site due to rain damaged roads but met with some folks there who will help lead the project. Back in the States we had a great response to our fundraising efforts. People couldn't quite believe that we could build houses for $750. As it turned out we got 18 units underway over the course of the next few months. This was at the height of the Maoist rebellion and those kind-hearted folks decided that we shouldn't be there. They closed down the project and kicked us out. Now we needed to regroup.

I returned to Nepal in January of 2007. The trip got off to a difficult start. The flight from Colorado Springs was cancelled so I got into Heathrow two hours late. Fortunately, the Jet Air flight to Mumbai was an hour late, so I was able to connect. I went to Mumbai to meet with TH Lawrence about starting a Fuller Center in India. The flight drama continued. From Mumbai I flew to New Delhi to catch a flight to Kathmandu. It turned out that Jet Air had dropped their 7:00 AM Delhi run so I had to take the 8:00 flight. This wouldn't have been a problem except that the flight was 90 minutes late, which wouldn't have been a problem except we landed at the domestic terminal and the flight to Nepal was leaving from the international one. The airport in Delhi is cleverly laid out so that to get from the domestic to the international terminal involves a 30-minute bus trip around the perimeter of the airport, pretty much assuring that I'd miss the Kathmandu flight and be stuck in India. Fortunately, my perverse luck held and the Royal Nepal Airlines flight, like all of the flights on this trip, was delayed, so my 34-hour battle with the airline industry ended in victory! I'm now ensconced in the Everest Hotel, a grand old dame of an inn that's very nice by my usual standard of international hostelry, but is sadly moving into its declining years. A little like me.

I met with our man on the ground, Samuel Tamang and Mr. BL Shrestha. They've put together a full week. BL is interested in doing something here in Kathmandu, but the costs will probably be prohibitive so Samuel is recommending a project in a rural area that's more in line with what we do, in a place called Trishuli.

9

We loaded into a Tata SUV—an Indian vehicle that looks like the offspring of a Land Rover and a Toyota. Trishuli is about 70 kilometers (41 miles to us old-timers) and it took a mere three hours to make the trip. It was an amazing journey into what they call the 'hilly' country. Except for the flora, which was semi-tropical, and the weather, which was fair, we could have been going over a mountain pass in Colorado. The drop-offs were exhilarating as we wound our way up one hill after another. We were in farm country and the hillsides were carved, top to bottom in an unending complex of terraces—row after row of sculpted farm land. The terraces were planted in a variety of crops—potatoes, mustard, radishes, onions, wheat. The fields are fed by streams that are intricately directed through them. I would like to have spent some time with one of the farmers, learning how it all worked. The scope of it was overwhelming—mile after mile of hillsides with a drop perhaps exceeding that of, say, Copper Mountain, all carved by man and beast. It has to be one of the great engineering and agricultural marvels on the planet.

Trishuli sits in a canyon between the terraced hills. We stopped first at the home of a local pastor, who holds services in the living room of his humble home. This is the congregation for whom Ascension Lutheran in Colorado Springs bought a piece of land for a church. We were warmly greeted and served hot buffalo milk, popcorn, of all things, and roasted soy beans. Not a bad treat actually. The milk had a wood stove flavor.

From there we walked down to the site where the new church will be built and then on to the home of another pastor, the senior pastor of the area with responsibility for six congregations. He's 35 years old and looks all of 25—I don't know how they do that! We went to the central church complex where I met with all of the local pastors and told them about The Fuller Center. There is great interest in our program. There are rumors afoot that there will soon be a change to the constitution that will allow for true religious freedom in the country. I warned the pastors to guard their gentle innocence if that comes to pass. This is my first experience with religious persecution and there is something very touching about how these Christians live their faith.

Next came lunch. I'm a guy who struggles with church suppers because I don't know whose kitchen the food comes from, so I'm always a little surprised at how I can eat whatever's put in front of me on these travels. We had chicken in an exotic sauce, spinach and white rice with *dhal*, a lentil soup that looks a lot like split pea. Then we got on the road for another three-hour trip back to Kathmandu

We spent time the next day visiting a couple of potential building sites and a number of government officials. The first site, Peace City, sits on the banks of the Bagmati River and is truly squalid. I have no idea how many live there, but it's a significant population. We then went to a neighborhood called Pathibhara, a squatter community that sits on dry land above the river and is a mix of daub and wattle shacks and brick and block houses. The people there have built a school and there's a small Christian church. We visited the home of the community association's secretary, a young man who makes a living as a trekker guide and by selling insurance and met with representatives of Lamentai, an NGO dedicated to improving the lot of the squatters. Both sites have significant problems for us. The people in Peace City can't or won't leave the area because it's close to work for many of them, though the next flood will help decide their fate. The folks in Pathibhara don't have legal title to the land. We keep finding obstacles to working in Kathmandu.

We then visited a number of government offices, including the Rural Housing Company, where we were met with a bouquet of flowers by the director (a good-guy Buddhist according to Samuel). We met with the Minister of Physical Planning and Works, who peppered me with questions and never gave me a chance to answer. Then on to the Chairman of the Rural Housing Board and the Secretary of the Ministry, both of whom are charged with keeping the wheels on the cart as ministers come and go. Samuel says that they're both Brahmin Hindus, which apparently limits their familiarity with honesty. You never know where these meetings might lead—seldom very far—but the courtesies were extended and we're at least on their radar. We got served tea or coffee everywhere we went except the last meeting, probably because Brahmins don't dine with us lesser beings.

We then went over to the Lion House, a colonnaded hulk that sprawls over 100 rooms and seven courtyards, built 100 years ago by an overwrought prime minister. From there it was back to the hotel and a fruitless effort to find a cyber café with working DSL and an unstuck keyboard. Aside from that frustration, and the veggie-burger I mistakenly ordered for dinner, it was a very good day.

The next day was a gentle one in Kathmandu. We visited one of BL Shrestha's projects—a four-unit townhome with two stories, the lower one with a living room, kitchen and bath, the upper with two bedrooms. He says that it can be built for $5,000 and will cost $7,500 with the land. As in so many urban areas land costs are prohibitively high. He showed us another site where the lots are less expensive but landlocked. Unless there's some legal provision for an access easement that site won't work either.

After the site visit we went to the home of Nil Shakyer, the general director of Rural Housing. What was meant to be tea turned into brunch with a potato and pea compote in a Nepali sauce, an omelet and tasty bread, sort of a flour *gordita*. I made an egg burrito with mine. Very pleasant. There was tea, of course. The recipe is 50% milk to 50% water brought to a boil. Then the tea leaves are dropped in and set to steep. At some point sugar is added—all of the tea and coffee I've been served here has been sweet. It was a lovely time with Mr. Shakyer and his family.

After tea we dropped BL off at home and Samuel and I visited the Monkey Temple—more properly the *Swayambhunath*. This is a collection of Buddhist and Hindu temples and monuments perched on a hill just outside of Kathmandu. As the name would indicate there are monkeys. Hundreds of them. The two religions have seemingly merged or, perhaps more correctly, Buddhism has adapted to allow for the Hindu pantheon. The rites and practices of both are a little pagan to a guy from Colorado, with a heavy dose of messy veneration of idols.

From the temples we went to Thamel, a shopping district that rose to importance during the hippie invasion of Nepal in the '60s. There I was left to my own devices. I bought some scarves and enjoyed the chaos. From there it was back to the Everest for a good night's sleep. Tomorrow we're off to Dhangadhi!

Dhangadhi is a city in the far west of the country and we're traveling there to visit a village that needs some help. Our 11:00 flight on Buddha Air from Kathmandu left at noon, continuing my run of delayed flights intact—six out of six so far. The flight was spectacular, though. We flew at 17,000 feet over a sea of clouds with the Himalayas rising above them in the distance—mile after mile of snowcapped peaks. We were met at the airport by a delegation from Rural Housing bearing flowers. I imagine that our fellow travelers, a couple of whom appeared to be westerners, were either impressed or confounded by the sight. We were taken to the Hotel Bidya where we were greeted by a statue of Ganesha, the Elephant God, and a large swastika over the door. Being a sophisticated traveler I know that this symbol is widely used in eastern and America Indian art. But being the son of World War II vets it's always a little bit jarring to actually see one in a public place.

We went down to Jugeda, a village a few miles south of Dhangadhi, where Rural Housing has a project. They provide families with land and some building materials and the families build their own houses. Most are small, daub and wattle structures with tin roofs. These are Tharu people with their own language, religion and traditions. Umesh, the local Rural Development officer, tells me that among the Tharu the custom is to put the kitchen in the northwest corner of the house and a shrine in the northeast. All of the houses have a grain storage bin built out of mud clay in the center of the house. The houses seemed adequate but fragile.

We went back to the Bidya where we had snacks—carrots, french fries, radishes and mutton tidbits—and watched a couple of movies that Nil, our brunch host from Kathmandu, was in. All I did was watch as they were in Nepali and the dialogue crept right past me. At about 9:00 we ate dinner around a campfire.

The next day we met with a number of organizations dedicated to improving the lot of very poor families who were, until it was outlawed, members of the bonded labor class. These are people who were obligated to work for the wealthy landowners and are barely above untouchables in the caste system. They are free now but their circumstances are dire. The groups we met with had names like Mukta Kamaiya Samaj and Tribhuvan Basi. I have little to report from these meetings as they were conducted in Nepali and there wasn't much translation going on. I did learn that there are over 13,000 former bonded families in need of housing and that the Tribhuvan Basi group just got back into their headquarters after being evacuated by the Maoist insurgency.

I got tea and flowers at every stop. Our transport, a Mahindra jeep, looked like a parade float before we were done with the trip—flowers everywhere. Speaking of the Jeep, it was quite the machine. Apparently Mahindra got a license to produce a jeep-like vehicle many years ago and it hasn't changed much over the years. Ours was a fairly new model and was everything a Jeep should be—sturdy, rugged and basic, the kind you can't get anymore. I would have loved to have brought one home.

From there we traveled to the focus of this trip, the village of Kankad. It's home to the Rara Tharu people, an indigenous tribe with its own language and culture. It's so far to the west that we actually had to go into India to get there. It's an unprotected border, so if I hadn't been told I wouldn't have known. We stopped at the school for more tea, flowers, and speechifying. We then walked over to the village, where we were very warmly received. More flowers! More tea! We were treated to a native dance in traditional costumes—colorful blouse and skirt combos with lots of embroidery mixed with spangles and small mirrors. There was a drummer and two boys who took turns singing a song of welcome and joy. And it was joyful.

We stopped by a house on the way in where a woman was weaving a reed mat, which I admired. Later, at the community meeting, she stepped forward and presented me with the mat! It was very touching. (I managed to get it home—we had quite the time with most of the staff of the Hotel Bidya helping wrap it up for the journey. Quite the event.)

We visited a couple of houses and, while they're not too substantial, being made of wattle and daub, they were amazingly tidy and clean. The whole village was that way—not a speck of litter anywhere and every house well-tended. The problem in this area is flooding, an annual event that often reaches the houses. The word *kankad* means sand, fitting for a community living on the river's banks. A second problem is overcrowding. The Rara Tharu live multi-generationally, and there can be as many as two dozen people living in a single, small house. The challenge we face is building sturdy, affordable houses that are large enough for these families

The people were very excited about the prospect of having new homes and expressed willingness to help build them and pay the costs, Fuller Center style. For its part Rural Housing has land on a bluff across the river with space for upwards of 100 houses. There are about 60 houses in the present village. If we were to build 100 houses for the community, we would improve the overcrowding by about half. A lot will depend on how well the community itself can get organized to move things along.

The trip is all but over. We made a courtesy stop at a place called Chaumala—more flowers—which is a village apparently built illegally on government land.

We're at the airport in Dhanghadi. Our flight left Kathmandu an hour and a half late. We called ahead so we had time to stop for lunch at a little street side café our driver knows. Not your typical tourist stop, but actually quite good. We had fried rice with onions and garlic, mustard greens and *dhal*, a type of lentil soup—all so tasty I had seconds.

We came across an interesting political situation at the airport. Apparently there's a Maoist bigwig flying in so there was a cadre of Maoist troops decked out in sharp green camo with bright red epaulets. But there were also regular army, armed police, and regular police and they're all milling around, chatting and acting like the last 10 years never happened. To make the picture complete a UN vehicle showed up as well. Interesting times. I tried to visit with the Maoists, who all seemed to be about 17. Their commander, an older woman, wasn't having anything to do with it and one by one she called the troops away. I wouldn't have learned much as none of them spoke English, but they were all pretty interested in this American who showed up in their midst.

Back in Kathmandu—it's Saturday, the Sabbath here, and I'm waiting for Samuel to pick me up for church. The U.S. must be one of the few places on earth that obsesses over timeliness. Bethel is Pentecostal and they pray in tongues, although when they're praying it's hard for my ear to tell tongues from Nepali. They're not as exuberant as the Nigerians, though, so the services are a little less scary.

After church we went for Thai food—very tasty. We then met with BL Shrestha and his board to talk about the future. I learned that there are some 35,000 families who were held captive by usury in the Dhangadhi area, many in a place called Chaumala, another stop on our tea and flowers tour out west. Outsiders had come in and loaned money secured by their land. The people were held in servitude due to the exorbitant interest that the loans carried. In the late 90s the government cancelled the debts and freed the bonded laborers but did not restore land ownership. Many of the people in Chaumala are squatting on government land and have not built permanent homes due to uncertainty of land tenure. Without some resolution to this issue Chaumala would not work for The Fuller Center.

Our focus, then, will be in Kankad. The land is available but needs to be surveyed and platted. We can start making bricks right away while we wait for the survey. There is the beginning of a community organization that can begin the process of family selection and start collecting down payments. This should be a great project.

I'm back in the airport waiting to take off for Delhi and parts west. The departure is delayed, completing the run—I'm now eight for eight on this trip. I have four flights left—can't wait to see how this turns out. The morning was one of high finance. For some reason I couldn't use my credit card to pay the hotel and the ATM wouldn't give me any cash—anxious to find out why. Finally, the good folks at Standard Chartered Bank gave me an advance. Nothing like being cashless in a foreign country—scary. I got enough to pay the hotel, the airport tax, and buy a cup of coffee. I'm on my way.

In Delhi—Jet Air made a gallant effort but couldn't quite pull off an on-time departure. I'm now 9 for 9.

EPILOGUE

I first traveled to Nepal in September of 2005. This was one of the two places that set The Fuller Center for Housing on the path to becoming a worldwide housing ministry. (The other was post-Katrina Shreveport.) I had been fascinated by that part of the world from my earliest memories, and visiting Kathmandu was a dream come true.

Nepal is a mystical place. From the moment you land, with pampas grass fronds waving their greeting, you know that adventure awaits. Kathmandu is an ancient city with Hindu temples and shrines at every corner. The Chinese destruction of Tibet has brought many Buddhists into the country, bringing their temples and customs as well. Visiting Nepal is like stepping back in time. Way back.

Nepal has changed since my first visit there. Just ten years ago the civil war with the Maoists was taking lives, the king was on his throne, and any Nepali who converted to Christianity was in violation of constitutional prohibitions. Today the war is over, the king has been deposed, and new laws allow for religious freedom. Nepal is a country with one foot in the Middle Ages and the other cautiously stepping into the 21st century.

It is one of the world's poorest countries. In the midst of ancient splendor can be found some of the worst housing conditions I've encountered. A quarter of the population lives below the poverty line and the need for decent housing was great before the 2015 earthquake struck. Samuel Tamang, our man on the ground there, reports that up to 90% of the houses in the central hill country have been destroyed. Trishuli, where we are working now and which was going to be the site of our 1,000th international house, is in the heart of the hill country or, as they call it there, the 'hilly' country.

Nepal's march into the modern age has been interrupted. It will take years to rebuild and The Fuller Center will be front and center getting families into simple, decent homes. Our work there has shifted from simple house building to disaster recovery and 100 families now have a simple, earthquake-resistant place to call home.

EL SALVADOR

December 2006

If anyone ever bothers to go through the journals I've kept of my travels they may be amused by how many begin with me sitting in the Colorado Springs airport. So I'm sitting in the Colorado Springs airport waiting for a flight to Atlanta. Tomorrow I leave for El Salvador for yet one more adventure. This one should be fun, not that the others haven't been, but I will at least be able to speak the language. Despite the claims of the Nigerians, the Nepalese and the Sri Lankans that they speak English I often find myself at sea when visiting with those folks. In El Salvador there will be no confusion—just Spanish. Or in my case, Mexican.

Now, I'm sitting in the airport in Atlanta waiting for my flight to El Salvador. I'm early, as usual, but I prefer it this way. All the check in and security business is behind me and I'd just as soon sit here as in some friendless hotel room. I get to San Salvador at about 1:00 PM their time, which is the same as Central time here, so I'll only be an hour ahead of home. I understand that someone from the government will meet me, walk me through customs and take me to the presidential lounge to wait for the rest of the party. There's not much going on today except for a planning meeting at dinner. Tomorrow we're scheduled for lunch with the First Lady and the rest of the week will be filled with tours of hospitals, orphanages and such.

I'm here with Jeff Cardwell and his Leadership Summit group. He makes this trip every year, inviting people who might be helpful to the work that his People Helping People Network is doing. Much of that work involves women's health issues and feeding programs. On the way from the airport to the hotel we stopped by a government orphanage for abandoned and orphaned children, many with severe handicaps. It's difficult to describe the feeling one has coming from a place of relative wealth, comfort and stimulation to see these kids whose lives are bound by bleak walls and, in some cases, a few square feet of crib space. We live most of our lives with little awareness of the tragedies that surround us.

The next day we traveled to Ahuachapán—little did I know how involved my life would become with that place. We visited the San José Hogar de la Niña, an orphanage for girls four to twelve years of age. It's run jointly by the Catholic Church and the government. The girls there have been orphaned or taken from their homes by the courts. They were a sweet bunch, some 38 in all. The nuns that tend to them were lovely and kind. The girls sang us some songs and gave us bread that they had baked and some embroidery from their sewing shop. Our docent was one of the older girls—Marjorie—and she became my friend. The sister who runs the place—they call her Sor—was delightful and it's clear that her goal is to provide a clean, safe and loving environment. But it's also clear that the girls long for the stability of a family and a loving relationship with a father. The goodbyes were hard. This is a place I'll return to.

In the afternoon we traveled to San Luis Talpa about an hour south of San Salvador. This is where the land is that Paul Lloyd may donate for house building. They measure the land in *manzanas* here and we weren't sure if we were looking at the one *manzana* that he was donating or at the four that he controls. Actually none of us were sure what a *manzana* is, so we were stumped. (Turns out that an El Salvadoran *manzana* is about 1.7 acres—not quite as much land as we thought we were looking at.) It looks like a good site—level with good access. There's a huge water tower there that was apparently damaged in the 2001 earthquake. There's also a well that looks to me to be functioning. We met two neighboring families—one lives just across the street. The lady of the house was making tortillas and I hoped she'd offer me one. Salvadoran tortillas are thicker than Mexican ones—more like *gorditas*. The wife of the other family is a seamstress—she gets $2.50 a shirt for school uniforms. Her husband is a mason and could become our first local employee. The boys showed up while we were there. They'd been fishing down at the beach, which is just a few miles down the road, and brought home their catch for dinner.

The next morning we had a breakfast meeting with Lisselot of the First Lady's office and Patty of the President's office to discuss a potential project. This was the key event of the week for me. We discussed their interests—housing for poor, single mothers—and the Fuller Center's methods and principles. It looks like something could develop from this. Next steps include finding some board members so we can set up a covenant partner. They have a long list of potential beneficiaries. Jeff Cardwell will sponsor the first house.

After the meeting I hunkered down to translate the partnership covenant while the rest of the group went to visit the burn unit at Bloom Hospital. This is a children's hospital and Jeff helped coordinate the funding to build the burn unit. They sent a car for me to meet them in San Sebastian, northeast of San Salvador, where I walked into a festival arranged to thank Jeff and his folks for their help to that community. I was escorted to the bandstand in the plaza where some speeches were made and they asked me to offer a prayer for the town. We then adjourned to City Hall for a giveaway. The *Secretaria de la Familia* brought gift packs of food and our team had toys to pass out. It was a nut act, as these things always are. We ran out of food and toys before we ran out of people, so they ushered us out the back door and we were on our way.

We left town for a hike in the country. I was never quite sure of the point of this expedition, but it apparently had to do with some tin that Jeff's group had funded to roof a house. We drove into the hills as far as we could and then hoofed it down a long, long hill to the house, which was made of metal sheets that replaced an adobe house that collapsed in the 2001 earthquake. As it happened we somehow left the homeowner and her kids back in town, so we couldn't see much and learned even less. She had quite a crew of ducks, geese and chickens and a pair of very loud but cowardly dogs. So, we stood around for a while, clucking sympathetically at the tragedy of it all, and then started the long, long climb back up to the van. As we neared the top we met the homeowner and her kids, who had managed to get a ride. Turned out she has seven kids, one an invalid. After the last one was born her husband left her. She makes a living by carrying bread that a neighbor bakes into town each day. We met another lady that day who rode up on an unruly horse, looking for help to rebuild her house. The horse kept us from getting too far into the conversation, which was good because we really didn't have anything to offer.

We headed back into San Sebastian to see how hammocks are made. As it happened we didn't get to see how hammocks are made but did visit an old, old building with a couple of looms, where they are making fabric by hand. One of the weavers has been doing this for forty years, every day, sitting there shuttling the threads back and forth, making cloth milli-inch by milli-inch. I had to buy a piece of his work, for which I was happy to pay full price.

We left San Sebastian for Cojutepeque, where we were supposed to have lunch. For mysterious reasons we passed on lunch and headed back to San Salvador. I didn't have breakfast and only a mid-morning cup of coffee, so I was a little peckish. I did manage to snag some dried coconut strips and a sort of molasses peanut brittle when we stopped for gas. No one wanted to share of my bounty, so I was able to stave off starvation. We ended up back at the Hilton and walked around the corner to Tony Roma's. Unbelievable—Tony Roma's. I need to start traveling with a more adventurous crowd. There was a sweet moment—shortly after we were seated there was a small temblor, which caused a lot of anxiety among the staff. The manager took them all into a side room where they held hands and said a prayer. That's something I wouldn't likely see back home.

Our last full day in El Salvador and we got off to a leisurely start. I opted for breakfast at McDonald's—$4 versus $14 at the hotel. We left town at about 10:00 heading for Lake Coatepeque to visit the *Castillo del Rey*—King's Castle. We spent a fair amount of time there, touring the facility, which is expansive, and learning about the ministry. The *Castillo*, I believe, is basically a school for missionaries and a base for their charitable work. They open it to volunteer groups, which is how Jeff got involved. One of the highlights of the trip was a visit to their Prayer Fortress. They have been praying there in shifts nonstop since 1998. They have dormitory rooms on the lower level, a small assembly area on the second, and the intercessionary prayer terrace on top.

I prayed for understanding. This is an Assemblies of God facility and it's hard for me to get my mind around their style of worship, especially the praying in tongues that some do. One of our team, a very wealthy businessman, enjoys sharing his spiritual gifts a little too much, which I found off-putting. So I prayed for understanding and got an immediate reply, "Don't worry about it. It just doesn't matter." That little bit of inspiration warmed my heart and soothed my troubled mind.

We went back to San Salvador and visited an arts and crafts mini-mall, where I picked up a few mementos. Then we went to an incredible mega-mall, where we were supposed to have dinner at yet another American restaurant. I was still full from our Burger King lunch, so I opted out.

I'm in the air now, heading home. I like El Salvador. It strikes me as a country that's reasonably happy with itself. It has very good roads and surprisingly little litter. Parts of San Salvador have the appearance of wealth—much of what I saw there looked like an upscale US city. The people are very friendly and courteous. There is clearly great poverty, but it doesn't reach out and slap you in the face the way it does in some places. I'd like to say something about the food but, alas, I didn't have a single Salvadoran meal during the entire trip.

The theme of the current government is *Un Gobierno con Sentido Humano*, which roughly translates A Government of Compassion. I think this will be a place where I'll spend some time.

March, 2007

I'm off to spend a little more time in El Salvador. This will be a short trip—I'll only be on the ground Monday through Wednesday and leave Thursday for home in time to unpack, repack and head off to Wilmington, North Carolina, for the Fuller Center board meeting. Sheilla's going to Wilmington with me, so that will be more fun.

The reason for this trip is to get a local organization in place to support the building project. Paul Lloyd has assembled a group of potential board members and we have a candidate or two. A second purpose of the trip is to get back to Ahuachapán to visit the orphans. Our friend Kathy Read has a needlework and stitchery shop and has given me a mountain of crafty stuff for the girls. I've got a suitcase full of knitting yarn, embroidery cloth and thread, and stamping supplies.

I'm lodging at the Hotel Berlin, a small inn near the US embassy. The owner is a former East German who has been in El Salvador for many years. I think. It was a little hard to follow his story. Apparently there's a Wal-Mart convention in town that has gobbled up all of the premium hotel space, which is why I'm not at the Hilton. Which is fine—it's always a little embarrassing to be staying in a place so far removed from what the people we're reaching out to live in.

Tuesday turned into a quiet day. Totally quiet. I was given the wrong contact phone number. I imagine that my voicemail messages were amusing to whomever they went to. When we finally connected we agreed to try to get to Ahuachapán later in the day. Left to my own devices I took a stroll to the *Las Cascadas* Mall. It looks close on the map but took me an hour to get there. Along the way I learned that San Salvador is not a pedestrian friendly place. I got to the mall sweaty and grouchy. I did get a phone, which has only rung once and that was when I called myself to hear what it sounded like. I bought a memory stick at an Office Depot of all places—the world is getting smaller and smaller. I took a cab back to the hotel—a five-minute ride. I spent the rest of the day translating orientation materials into Spanish. A lonely day on the lonely planet.

The purpose of this trip is to work on plans to start building on the land that Paul Lloyd wants to donate for housing. We did start talking about forming a local board and making arrangements for Trish—our project leader—to get her truck and tools into the country. With that settled we're about to start building.

We did make it up to Ahuachapán. The girls were delighted with the bounty I left them.

January 2008

Another trip south, an important one this time. I think our time with Paul has run its course. His vision for the site is to build houses as giveaways for single mothers—a noble undertaking but not our approach. I thought we'd already worked through this and come to agreement about the program but I was apparently wrong. This, coupled with the fact that Trish and Paul do not get along, argues for a change. We met with Paul's group and let them know that we were pulling out and started the search for a new site. There was some urgency to this as we were planning to hold the Millard and Linda Fuller Build here later in the year.

We found a nice parcel in a place called Santa Clara just outside of San Luis Talpa and near to the Lloyd site. They wanted $19,000 for it, which is about the going rate. We had it checked out and there weren't any title issues. Since we weren't yet established as a legal entity in El Salvador I had to purchase the land in my own name, so I am now a proud property owner there.

Traveled back to Ahuachapán to visit the orphanage. Sor Guillermina was away so Sor Imelda received me. I had a good bit of yarn for the orphan girls. It turns out that their cistern is failing and she asked if we could come up with $600 to repair it. I promised to work on it.

Back then to San Salvador to meet with Jaime Saca at his Hiper Europa store. He was disappointed that things didn't work out with Paul but wants to continue to be supportive. Hiper Europa is a lot like Walmart, so much so that I believe it became a Walmart store in later years.

March 2008

Back to El Salvador. Sheilla is with me this time. We're leading a small work team from Ascension Lutheran Church. I'll spend as much time as I can with them, building away, but have some serious administrative tasks, like getting the permitting issues resolved on the land, getting a legal entity in place, and getting the plans together for the big build next fall. All of this on top of getting over the guilt for being bumped to business class and leaving Sheilla in coach. They wouldn't let me switch with her but did sneak her drinks. Awkward.

We got to San Salvador and down to the beach house around two, settled in there and checked out the guest house just down the beach from us where the Ascension folks will stay. Had dinner at La Dolce Vita in La Libertad. A good start to the week. I'll recount the rest of the week in blog posts.

THE GREAT SALVADORAN WORK CAMP ADVENTURE—March, 2008

My wife Sheilla and I are heading to El Salvador on a Fuller Center work camp. In my many years in this work I have led a good number of major building events and I've welcomed hundreds of work campers to building sites, but I've never been on a work camp as a volunteer. Until now. Well... almost. As I'm an administrator I'll have to spend a fair amount of time administrating. The Millard & Linda Fuller Build will be held in El Salvador the week of November 17. We'll build 10 houses in a week, so there's a good deal of preparation to be done.

Anyway, we're off to El Salvador where we'll spend Spring Break building with a group from Ascension Lutheran Church in Colorado Springs. Getting from the Springs to San Salvador is a little tricky—the cheapest flights seem to have schedules that require you to spend the night either in the Denver airport or in Atlanta. We opted for Atlanta, so here we are, nestling into our motel room, and getting excited about the week ahead.

We'll get to San Salvador at noon tomorrow, Easter Sunday. Our project director, Trish Stoops, will pick us up for the 20-minute drive to the Fuller Center compound at Las Flores, located right on the Pacific seashore. Las Flores is close to the airport as well as our building site and just a half hour from San Salvador, making it an ideal hub for our activities.

I'll keep jotting notes about this adventure and posting them through the week to the extent our internet access at Las Flores allows. We're looking forward to a great adventure.

DAY ONE- GETTING READY—We're in El Salvador now. Sheilla & I came in a day ahead of the Ascension group. It was a hard day in paradise—getting groceries, eating seafood, checking out the Pacific to make sure it was up to par. We're pretty much exhausted.

This is a great place for work camps and we hope to host many of them. The people are incredibly warm and friendly, the countryside is lush, and it's exotic enough to offer a true international experience. Tomorrow we may do some actual work. But then again, we may just have to do a little more planning.

In the "it's an amazing world" category I just got an email from Joe O'Brien of The Fuller Center-Brazzaville. (These communications marvels continue to amaze those of us who grew up with dial telephones.) He wrote to say that the group from Engineering Ministries International (eMi) had arrived to start work on planning the new village we are going to build at Makana. eMi is a great organization that solves engineering problems for other nonprofits around the world. We are delighted to have them with us in the Republic of the Congo.

Time now to rest from my labors. The only problem with working in places like this is that it's hard to tell if you're really working!

DAY 2—More planning today. We did actually have some meetings, but in the true spirit of committee work, not a lot of actual work got done. The Ascension group arrived at noon. They'd been traveling since 9:00 last night, so they were a little bushed. A dip in the sea and a run down the shore brought renewed energy to the under 30 set. The rest of us got tired just watching. There are six in their group, Tiffany Malcom, Rex & Meg Rudy, Aaron Holt, Jenna Dolata and Kathy Mannerberg. We've been joined by a couple of new friends, Jake & Sophie, who have been touring Central America by volunteering from place to place.

We knew that the group would be a little tuckered out from their travels, so our goal was to get them acclimated, fed and rested. We accomplished all of that so we can count the day a success. Special mention needs to be made of the feeding part—our program assistant, Carmen Gallardo, happens to be a professional chef and she whipped us up a paella to die for. Given the accommodations, the views and the food this is a work camp experience that will be hard to top. Tomorrow we get to work.

DAY 3—Today we worked, and it felt great. We're between projects here. We had to step back from the work we'd started earlier at Saint Joe's and don't have all of the permits to start work yet at the new site at La Moras de Santa Clara in San Luis Talpa. We have a crack construction crew down here and wanted to keep them busy. As we've gotten to know them all better we've learned that most of them live in houses that qualify them for our program. So, during our hiatus between initiatives we've been doing some Greater Blessing work on their houses. Charity, they say, begins at home, so we're taking care of our own while we wait for the paperwork to take care of others.

This week we're working on the house of our superintendent, Pedro Chicas. Pedro and his wife Bacilia have three kids—Josue (11), Melissa (9) and Alexi (2). They live in a one room block house with few facilities, so we're adding on a couple of rooms and an indoor bath. Today we mixed mortar, laid blocks, cut and shaped rebar and made a big dent in the project. The masons were impressed, if not by our skills, by our willingness to do whatever had to be done. It was a great day of work—not too hot, good company, fruitful work and a great spirit. For those of us who spend our time in administrative efforts, as important as those efforts might be, it was a great blessing to end the day with dirty hands and a sweaty brow. We had another wonderful dinner thanks to Carmen and Yolanda but had a delayed start because a huge sea turtle had come ashore to lay eggs and we had to check it out. Some local folks were protecting her so we couldn't get too close. They said that once the eggs were laid we could return, so we ate and then rushed back to watch the new mama head back to sea. Apparently, sea turtles aren't burdened with maternal instincts. By all appearances her parenting duties were done. It was a great thing to be a part of though.

Everyone seems to be acclimated and un-jet-lagged, so spirits are running high. Tomorrow we should get the floors in and the rest of the walls raised. If the roof gets put on Thursday we'll be close to done. What a ministry—house by house, one house at a time, we are able to be a part of a life-changing experience, not just for the family that will live in the house, but for the good souls who give of their time and talents to make it possible. What a blessing!

DAY 4—We had another great day at the worksite today, Wednesday. We got the gable ends done and purlins painted so the roof can go up on Thursday. We also dug out the pits for the septic tank and settling pond, two holes both seven feet deep. I say we, but it was actually the kids that got that work done. Sheilla and I realized that we are the true elders on this site, and even though that distinction doesn't seem to carry a lot of weight, we used it to keep ourselves above ground.

There's a good spirit with this work camp. The Ascension folks and our new friends Jake and Sophie have been real troopers, taking on any task with cheer. The only times people have been edgy is when they didn't get an assignment—something that gets quickly remedied. The Chicas family has been hard after it as well, along with their extended family which appears to be quite extensive. A couple of the team members know a word or two of Spanish and Jake & Sophie are fluent, so we've been able to communicate well. We took everyone in to San Luis Talpa for lunch at this great little buffet. Sheilla and I had rice, beans, chiles rellenos, tortillas and a drink for $3 each—not a bad deal.

We had a pleasant evening of surf and sand and another gourmet meal. The surf here is quite good I'm told by those who know about such things. It's a little brutal for the uninitiated, though, and I worry about the kids, but they seem to be up to the challenge and we haven't lost anyone yet. I'm sure this will be of great comfort to any parents who may be checking these postings out.

Tomorrow is a rest day. We're going up to Ahuachapán to visit the orphans. There are some pyramids along the way so we'll have a chance to play tourist and rest up a bit for Friday, which will be a big day.

DAY 5—We try to make time during our work camps for the volunteers to experience the local culture. Today was our day, and a great day it was. We left La Libertad at 10:00 after paying the phone bill, finding the post office and buying $62 worth of diesel. The trip from La Libertad to San Salvador is a hike—I'd guess that you gain about 2000 feet in elevation in 35 kilometers. We're driving a Kia Pregio, which is a nice piece of machinery. Sheilla and I drove it up to San Salvador earlier in the week and zipped up the mountain. With nine passengers the going was a little slower today, and we were one of those vehicles that the rest of us are generally irritated with—crawling up the inclines and then speeding on the downhill to get enough oomph to make the next climb.

We made it to San Salvador without causing too much grief, skirted the city, and headed northwest towards Ahuachapán, a 100-kilometer trip. There's an orphanage there that Jeff Cardwell and DJ Bakken introduced me to a couple of years ago, and I've visited it on every trip since. It's home to 50 girls, ages 2 to 13, who for a variety of reasons have no other place to live. Given the inherent sadness of such a place it's really very pleasant. It's run by nuns who show the girls great love and try to give them a leg up in life by teaching them sewing, embroidery, knitting and baking, and we brought them a suitcase load of supplies. This trip we also brought money collected from a number of friends to help them rebuild their cistern, which was damaged in last summer's storms and has left them without a steady supply of water. I was able to raise the money for the repairs. One of the donors is the 8-year-old granddaughter of Fuller Center Board member Marlene Muse, who wanted to give a meaningful gift to someone in need for her birthday.

Our time at the orphanage was golden. The Ascension folks romped and played with the girls and took hundreds of photos, each of which had to be closely inspected. How they've ever learned about the marvels of digital photography is beyond me. Then the girls sang us a couple of songs and we had to take our leave. It's a hard place to say goodbye to.

We then drove to Chalchuapa to visit the Tazumal pyramid. This is a structure that was built and rebuilt over the centuries with influences from the Olmeca, the Maya and the Toltec peoples. Amazingly it wasn't discovered until 1942, and a good deal of work has been done since then to restore it. It was a fascinating stop and worth the visit.

We visited an artisans' market in San Salvador on our way through town and everyone picked up a treasure or two. Then on to Mr. Donut where, despite the name, we had a true Salvadoran repast. Fuller Center friends Maria and Mario Cruz joined us there to talk about the future of The Fuller Center in El Salvador.

Tomorrow Sheilla & I leave for home. It's been a wonderful week of memory making. We'll miss the people and the places and look forward to our next visit with fond anticipation.

October 2008

Back in El Salvador to make sure everything is on track for the big build next month. We had to part company with Trish, and that's been messy. We have found a new project director, a man named Mike Bonderer, who came to El Salvador a few years back to die and just keeps living. He's built a number of houses here using a system of metal forms into which the concrete walls are poured. We'll probably use it later on but as the work has started with block we'll use that for the work week.

November 2008

The Millard and Linda Fuller Build is underway! We have some 180 volunteers here. Most are staying at a place called Estero y Mar, a lovely resort on the beach some 20 minutes from the work site. Great progress was made on 10 houses—the families will move in soon. In addition to the build we had a board meeting (interrupted by a small earthquake that served to keep everyone awake for the balance of the meeting). Mike did a great job of pulling things together—amazing, actually, considering the short time he had.

EPILOGUE

El Salvador has become one of the Fuller Center's most productive partners, with 355 families now in decent homes. Many of these are due to the generosity of New Story Charity, a Silicon Valley based nonprofit that raises money for groups like ours to use for house building. They have a special interest in large-scale projects, so we have built a neighborhood of 91 houses with them in Nuevo Cuscatlán, just outside of San Salvador, and two other projects totaling 146 houses in Ahuachapán, the site the girls' home I visited so often. (Sadly, that home is no longer operating—the government withdrew their support in an apparent effort to consolidate services. Alas.)

Work in San Luis Talpa stalled after the death of Mike Bonderer. We are looking at ways of revitalizing the program there with help from our partner organization in El Salvador, the local branch of Jeff Cardwell's People Helping People network.

NIGERIA & GHANA

THE TATTERED PASSPORT

February, 2006

I'm in Atlanta waiting for the plane to Dulles. From there I'll go to Amsterdam, then Kano, and then Abuja, where I'll be about 24 hours from now. I don't know what to expect. I've done some research and it seems that Nigeria might not be a garden spot. But I'm up for the challenge.

I got into Abuja around 9:00 PM on Sunday and was met by our man on the ground, Sam Odia. A long trip, although I spent as long in the Amsterdam airport as on either flight. I'm staying at the Angelus Hotel in the Garki District—not 5 star but not bad. I have a computer in my room, so I don't feel too disconnected. I can get on the internet and send emails—it's an amazing world.

The food's not bad. I've only had a couple of meals so far—yams and eggs for breakfast yesterday and spaghetti Bolognese last night—an interesting dish with shredded beef rather than ground.

We had a couple of good meetings yesterday, one with Mrs. Roke Omame, the Special Assistant to the President for housing, Dr. Mimiko, the Minister of HUD and John Alkuli, the Permanent Secretary of HUD. Not a bad crowd for our purposes. The result, I think, is that the government is about to give us some 40 acres of partially developed land. I think, I say, because I'm having a little trouble keeping up with the local patois. English is the lingua franca here, but an interesting English it is.

So far Nigeria reminds me a little of Mexico. Abuja has the feel of a big Tijuana. Even the smells are alike. When I stepped out of the air terminal I was taken back to Mexico City. Abuja is less frantic, congested and dirty than New Delhi. I'm told that Lagos is a little different—I'll know soon.

I had dinner last night at the home of the Housing Minister—an honor I believe. This is a man who travels in a chauffeured car with a chase vehicle and four heavily armed guards. His house is across the street from the old US embassy. He seems to be a man of action and is very interested in working with us. I suspect that his level of interest will correlate with our ability to perform.

We traveled to Lagos today on Bellview Airlines. It was reminiscent of old-time flying. We did have our bags checked through an x-ray machine but that was pretty much the extent of security. They didn't even ask for identification. This laxity could be connected to the warning signs they used to have in US airports about traveling to Lagos. The aircraft—one a Boeing, the other an Airbus—had seen service in Poland and the Balkans respectively based on the signage and safety cards. They tell me that most of the cars in the country are used from Europe. (Except for Peugeots, which are made there—the 504 is Africa!)

We got to Lagos at 9:00 PM and went directly to the hotel—the Westside Inn. It's a little nicer than the Angelus although the room is smaller, the TV doesn't work, and the restaurant doesn't open until 7:00 in the morning. So I'm sitting here in my room trying to decide if I should drink the Viju Milk I found in the mini-bar, but I'm not sure what it is.

We spent the first day here in the car. The air conditioner broke down about a third of the way through the trip, so it was a hot and windy day. We went to Ota, where the President has a farm—Nigeria's Crawford, Texas. From there we went to Abeokuta where we met with the Commissioner of Housing and the Principal Secretary. We had good meetings and I can see us working there someday. We continued north to Ibadan to the home of Sam's in-laws where we had lunch. We then visited the Development Policy Centre, which was founded by Sam's late father-in-law. The PDC is a think tank that works on public policy. It was a good trip and nice to be in the countryside after experiencing the huge urban sprawl of Lagos.

Sam is a mover and shaker and will surely be a force for affordable housing in Nigeria. I hope we can keep up. Among his plans is one to have a separate for-profit construction entity that would help fund the Fuller Center work.

General impressions—I found Nigeria to be a much less fearsome place than I was prepared for. Corruption is a widely acknowledged fact of life—every conversation includes mention of it. There is, however, a concerted campaign afoot to reduce corruption in both the private and public sectors. Three state governors are currently under indictment and the federal government seems to be working hard to clean itself up. The government is well aware of the reputation the country has overseas thanks to the Nigerian 'princes' who prey on the susceptible with promises of wealth—there's a billboard campaign against them.

Homeownership is becoming a government and private sector priority. The government encourages homeownership through a mandatory investment program into the National Housing Fund by way of a payroll deduction for all employees in the formal economy—a little like Social Security in the States. These funds can then be accessed by the taxpayer for down payments and guaranteed mortgages, at least in theory. There is great need in Nigeria for decent housing.

We will most likely be building in the 'para-urban' suburbs of Abuja where many of the city's lower level workers live.

Sunday morning and I'm at breakfast. My new staple is oatmeal and tea—who would have thought? Sam will pick me up soon for church. We're going to the first service which is apparently shorter because they have to make room for the second service. I'm looking at two hours of speaking in tongues and general rambunctiousness. Ah, the variety of the Christian experience. I have my little pocket Bible with me at these services so I can cover my lack of zeal with the appearance of studiousness. Today's service was a little more conventional than the Wednesday night event, which was basically a prayer meeting in tongues. Today's started in tongues but then moved into the singing of the Nigerian national anthem—a nice touch. Then more praying and singing and building frenzy.

There was a sermon, but the pastor's accent is so thick and he speaks so quietly that I couldn't understand one word in three. It had something to do with men treating their wives well in honor of Valentine's Day. The pastor is quite personable and, based on the reactions of the crowd, very funny. I couldn't understand the jokes. After the service the visitors were taken to the pool area (the church meets in a hotel) and encouraged to be faithful and come to the Wednesday night meetings as well as another on Tuesday, the purpose of which got past me. When I was able to explain that I really was a visitor from afar (in case they might not be able to tell) and would be leaving town later that day they relented and simply welcomed me.

After church we went to Sam's for Sunday dinner. It was quite good. I haven't been too taken with Nigerian cuisine. Manioc yams are a big part of the diet—large, which are melon-like things that have been pretty tasteless in the two forms I've had them, boiled and pounded. The pounded version comes to the table looking like a big ball of mashed potatoes tightly encased in saran wrap with what they call soup but is more like spinach mush. That wouldn't be so bad except they cook it with chips of dried fish that are supposed to reconstitute in the cooking, but in my experience, don't.

It's been a great week. I've only had one unhappy experience—they charged me $20 at the inn in Lagos because their faulty key broke off in my door. They wanted $40, but I controlled my irritation and graciously bargained them down. At the same inn I had my first encounter with a 'professional' woman who thought

I looked in need of company. I declined, hurried into my room, and double locked the door.

Some observations—Abuja is a western-style city. It has the benefit of being young and planned. It was designed specifically to be the national capital and sits right in the middle of the country and right on the imaginary line that separates the Muslim north from the Christian south. In the center of the city is a large plaza with a huge mosque facing a huge Christian church—a public nod to national unity. A major investment has been made in roads—there are divided highways and boulevards everywhere, which give the city a more open and healthy feel than, say, Lagos. The streets in Lagos are a mess. Lagos is like a poorer Mexico City. It's huge, out of control and dirty. What I didn't see in Lagos were the attractive colonias you find tucked into the corners of Mexico City.

The people here—especially the serving people—are courteous almost to a fault. They say 'sorry' instead of 'oops' or 'bless you' if you trip or sneeze. I've been called 'master' more than once—a little disconcerting. Sam tried to carry my bags again and I told him that we Americans weren't accustomed to being served to which he advised that Nigerians are taught from an early age not to allow 'the elderly' to tote. 'The elderly!' He tried to atone by saying that anyone my age or older is considered elderly but, alas, the damage was done. (I later learned that life expectancy for men in Nigeria is 53 years of age, so, at the ripe old age of 57, I guess I really was elderly.)

I'm in Amsterdam now, waiting for the flight to Atlanta. It's hard to believe that I was in this same place just over a week ago. What an adventure! All of my careful planning for who knows what sort of medical or physical trauma I might suffer proved unnecessary. Except for being extorted by the hotel in Lagos over the broken room key I experienced no crime. I never used the water filter or mosquito repellant. The shots were for diseases I probably wasn't exposed to, but who knows? No G.I. problems, no cold, no flu. I'm returning a whole person with a much higher level of confidence for my next trip.

October 2006

I left Colorado Springs yesterday afternoon for Minneapolis, then on to Amsterdam. I slept some on the plane but always feel a little foggy when I get to Schiphol. I've flown on Northwest Airlines so far—second rate aircraft, food and service. I'm on KLM to Abuja so things should improve. Continental and Delta both do a better job than Northwest. I got into Abuja late, went straight to the hotel to find the restaurant closed. I'm a hungry boy, but morning is coming and breakfast with it. I woke to the alarm, got up, brushed my teeth, shaved and turned on the water heater. Then I realized that it was only 3:30 in the morning. Turns out that the power went off and before the generator kicked in the smoke alarm went off. I left the water heater on for the luxury of a hot shower first thing in the morning. I hope it doesn't blow up.

Today is the day we dedicate the new Fuller Center office. It's very attractive with shingled awnings over the interior doors and plenty of space for meetings and training sessions. The dedication was nicely done. The President's assistant for housing was there along with representatives from the army, USAID, Ecobank and Oceanic Bank. We then had a board meeting with the entire board present. One member, Archbishop Fearon, heads the Anglican Province of Kaduna in the Muslim north and is internationally acclaimed for his efforts in creating better Muslim-Christian relations.

We then traveled to the site of the first Fuller Center houses at Luvu-Madaki to the east of Abuja. There will be a 20-unit neighborhood here, built out of concrete blocks manufactured on site. They will have a common room, kitchen and bath and cost less than $2,500, placing them well within the reach of those who have no other access to homeownership. Under The Fuller Center-Nigeria's incremental housing program the purchase of one of these small starter homes is the first step to adequate but affordable housing. After the three-year mortgage is paid homeowners can sell the house back to The Fuller Center and use the proceeds as the down payment on a larger unit. An interesting approach.

The next day we left for the airport late and caught the flight to Port Harcourt—barely. (They pronounce it something like Potárco). It was a race to the finish, especially because our Aero flight had been cancelled and we were squeezed onto a Sosoliso flight. We made it. Port Harcourt is in the Delta region, Nigeria's oil fields. We're here for meetings with Shell about a project they have in mind. They put us up at the Novotel—high luxury in the bush! A night here with meals comes in at $230—I pay $79 at the Angelus. Fortunately Shell is picking up the tab

The meeting with Shell was interesting. Their headquarters in Port Harcourt is like a military camp under siege—understandable given the rebel situation in the South. What we're working on is essentially a consulting agreement to determine the cost of relocating nine families who will lose their homes to a new pipeline. Negotiations have been going on long enough to cause a time crunch—the pipeline goes in next March. Apparently everyone has agreed to the contract terms and

35

Shell is set to cut a check next week for 80% of the cost of the evaluation. Sam and company can then get the analysis done and it's likely that they'll get the construction contract as well. This is all a little unorthodox, but it's okay I think because it accomplishes three things: (1) it provides a way to test the construction system and technology for free; (2) it will provide The Fuller Center Nigeria with some income; and (3) it puts us on Shell's radar for possible future funding. And then, of course, it provides decent housing to nine families who are about to be dislocated.

We left then for Lagos, getting in at about 3:00 in the afternoon. Billy, our driver, suggested that we try a different hotel as the Westwood, the place that ripped me off over a broken room key, was getting a reputation for lax security. Imagine that. So we ended up at Knightbridge, a fairly new but rather bleak inn. They had food and I ordered fish and chips. I asked if they were English style and he assured me that they were. What I got was half of a fried fish and French fries, but it was very tasty.

We spent the next day driving around Lagos. The traffic there is the worst I've ever seen. We visited executives at Oceanic Bank and Citibank. We may be able to do something with them, especially Oceanic.

We got to the airport at 5:00 PM for an 8:00 flight but were able to rebook on the 5:30. My ticket almost didn't clear, but finally did. With another mad dash, we were underway. Almost. An hour and a half into a 50 minute flight it was clear that something was amiss and I knew we were in trouble when the tower sent a car out to find out why we weren't taking off. We finally did and later learned from our driver that a bad storm had blown through. I don't know why we never heard anything from the cockpit—could be that the pilot didn't speak English. All we heard from him were curt messages to the flight attendants that sounded like Dutch. But we're here and safe. There was another State Department email waiting for me warning against travel to Port Harcourt. I must have had a guardian angel in tow.

We spent the next day touring Abuja. We travelled through the federal government complex—very impressive. You can't get close enough to the Legislative Assembly or the Presidential Villa to see much. We did get into the National Church—a space age cathedral in the center of town. We didn't try to get into the National Mosque. We went into the hills high above town but it wasn't clear enough to see much. What was interesting was a group of workers who were skimming off a 12-inch layer of granite from the top of a hill by hand. We also met a group of local tribeswomen, the Gwari, who were fashioning wooden devices that they used to carry things on their heads and huge bowls made out of calabash gourds.

January, 2008

I'm back at the Angelus Hotel in Abuja—flew in today from Kinshasa. I left Jim Conway at 6:00 this morning to catch a Hewa Bora flight scheduled for a 9:15 departure. It left at 10:15, stopped in Cameroon for an hour, and got me into Lagos at 3:00. I then took a Virgin Nigeria flight to Abuja. Their credit card machine wasn't working so I had to dig into my precious reserves. The Abuja flight was scheduled for 4:30 in the afternoon, left at 5:15 and got me there at 6:15. The good news is that yet one more set of flights is behind me.

We had meetings the next morning at Ecobank. There is a lot of creativity going on here—I'm not sure how some of it will fit our model. We talked about using bank loans for those who could afford them. They would be interest bearing. We'd use Fuller Center zero interest loans for the rest. I worry that combining the two systems in a single project will result in jealousies developing. The homeowners will surely compare their situations. We followed that with a board meeting where many of my concerns were raised by other members. This will be an interesting project to follow.

We also spent time talking about in-country fund raising. The way they've set things up they'll have relatively large administrative costs, and while we can support some of it we'd rather see the money we send go into house building. We did wrestle the truck issue to the ground—they agreed to raise $5,000 which I agreed to match and they'll buy what they can afford.

We started early the next day for a site visit and work day. We spent the morning laying block. My first assignment was to tote the block and then I got promoted to the mortaring crew. We did fair work. At about 11:00 they brought us a snack—a variety of fried, stuffed breads—but I thought it was lunch, which would come an hour and a half later. So I over-ate the appetizers and skipped lunch.

Just before lunch we dedicated the second set of ten houses. All of the homeowners were represented and it was nice to get a little closer to the results of our work. We then had a family meeting and headed back to town. A good day.

We got back to the office at about 3:00 and I met with a woman who came over from Sierra Leone to discuss starting The Fuller Center there. She told me that she'd been trying to get our attention for two years without success. I'll check that out when I get home—I don't have any recollection of contacts from there. There's something about her that doesn't quite sit right with me—not sure what, but I wasn't excited by my time with her. (That turned out to be a portent of things to come!) I told her that we were in a period of consolidation and might not be naming any new international covenant partners for a while. I did agree to send her some information. I would have printed it then and there but the lights went out.

A quick note about the skies here, which are generally hazy this time of year. It's due to what they call *harmattan,* winds that bring dust from the Sahara into central Africa.

Tomorrow I'm off to Ghana. When I got to the airport in Accra I searched for a friendly face. The custom in most of the developing world is for international arrivals to be met by a multitude. Since I didn't know my hosts I didn't know who to look for. Many of the waiting folks had signs and I looked in vain for one that said David or Snell. As it turned out I stood out in the crowd and finally heard my name being called. My host was carrying a sign, but it bore his name—Jones—instead of mine. Go figure.

Jones and his buddy Alex took me to the guest house where I would stay—very nice. I ordered egg fried rice, which seemed like a gentle meal. It was, but huge—I brought half of it home. Jones and Alex ordered bush meat. Bush meat, the best I can gather, is anything from the jungle that moves on its own. I passed.

The next morning we drove a couple of hours north of Accra to the village of Agomeda, where there is land for house building. We stopped along the way to meet with the District Administrator, who was gracious but clearly not expecting us. Jones said something about not being able to confirm a time because of uncertainty about my schedule. Strange, I thought, as he'd had my itinerary for several weeks.

We then went to the potential building site. The owner wasn't home, again due to the uncertainties of my travel plans precluding a firm appointment. Maybe in Ghana time keeping is sufficiently random that they really weren't sure of my itinerary. Who knows? It's a nice site—level and ample, although we don't know the exact size. The District Administrator did offer the services of his surveyor. I asked about the owner's motivation in giving us the land and was told that once the families are paying their mortgages he would be given a token gift. I couldn't get answers to a couple of key questions: how much will the token gift be; and will we have clear title to the land before we start building. These seem to be reasonable questions.

We had a gentle Saturday morning. We're going to have a board meeting here at the Inn and then take a trip into town. The meeting started at 12:45 with Jones, Alex, Eric and Gideon. Jones is clearly the visionary. Alex is a friend of Jones and has a car, so he's our driver. He's also the president of the PTA at the high school. Eric is an architect and came up with the house plans. Gideon is a Pentecostal pastor who was mostly concerned about a wedding he was missing. I gave my spiel—business plan, budget, committees, etc. and agreed to provide some templates. They already have many of our materials but haven't yet looked at them. They asked again about money for administration and explained how hard it would be to raise money locally. I'm always a little worried when there's more concern with money for administration than for building.

Sunday I was left to my own devices. I was warned against going out of the Inn. Apparently the Africa Cup soccer finals are being played today here in Accra. It was a long, long day. The guys agreed to pick me up early on Monday to get me to the airport. They were an hour late and I was getting testy. The airport was packed with all of the soccer revelers heading home. The check in line went clear to the street and I was scarcely halfway there when my flight time arrived. Fortunately I was flying Virgin Nigeria, which is always late by an hour so I made it.

From Accra I went back to Lagos for one final flying adventure. I got to Lagos mid-morning for an evening flight. In Africa they don't open the ticket counter until a couple of hours before the flight and you can't get past security until you've cleared the ticket counter, so I was facing a long day in the somewhat inhospitable entry area of the terminal. I found a restaurant on a bridge that overlooked the ticket counter so I settled in. I ordered a hamburger but apparently my mental conversion chart failed me—when the ticket came it was for $26!

The ticket counter finally opened and so I scurried down only to learn that they didn't have a reservation for me on the flight. My ticket agent had done yeoman's work in getting me around Africa, but failed on my exit. They ended up taking me to the Air France office deep in the bowels of the terminal and I was able to get my ticket agent on the phone. He spent a few suspenseful minutes chatting with the Air France folks and, voilà, a reservation appeared.

Traveling in Africa is not easy, and as I look back on this trip I wonder how I survived it. Here's the flight plan:

- Colorado Springs to Atlanta on Delta
- Atlanta to Paris on Delta
- Paris to Brazzaville on Air France
- Brazzaville to Mbandaka on UNHCR aircraft
- Mbandaka to Kinshasa on UNHCR aircraft
- Kinshasa to Lagos on Hewa Bora
- Lagos to Abuja on Virgin Nigeria
- Abuja to Lagos on Virgin Nigeria
- Lagos to Accra on Hewa Bora via Cameroon
- Accra to Lagos on Virgin Nigeria
- Lagos to Paris on Air France
- Paris to Atlanta on Air France
- Atlanta to Colorado Springs on Delta

Never again.

EPILOGUE

Our work in Nigeria has followed a somewhat different path. Sam Odia, who heads up our work there, is a Millard Fuller-style entrepreneur, dedicated to the cause of affordable housing and always on the lookout for new ways of providing it. The original project there—The Fuller Center Housing Estate—housed 97 families. More recently, though, much of his work is just outside of The Fuller Center's program, using interest bearing financing and government funds, and in this work another 600 families now have a decent place to call home. He has become a person of consequence for his housing work.

SRI LANKA

July, 2006

It's 8:00 in the morning in London. I left home 13 hours ago and have two more legs on this trip. I'm tired but don't dare sleep for fear of missing my flight to Dubai which will make me miss my flight to Colombo. From the Springs to Colombo will be a 34 hour trip. I did get bumped to first class for the Dubai flight and I was able to get some sleep.

I arrived in Colombo at 9:15 local time. Passport and customs were a breeze and Pastor Ranjan Fernando, our man on the ground here, picked me up and, two hours later, we're in Moratuwa, south of Colombo. He has a large home. He lives on the first floor with his wife and his daughter and upstairs has his office and dormitory space. I'm in a single room with its own bath—not plush but very pleasant and appropriate to my new missionary lifestyle. After a restful afternoon we went to the 200th anniversary celebration of the Mt. Livinia Hotel. Lots of food and drink and 2,000 of Colombo's finest—a great start to the trip.

Ranjan heads the United Christian Fellowship, a nondenominational church and NGO that serves a number of needs in and around Moratuwa. Their activities include an orphanage, medical and feeding programs and evangelism. We had a breakfast meeting the next morning with 25 of his board members and associates to start talking about The Fuller Center's work in Sri Lanka. Many are former Habitat volunteers and two are former HFH staff members. It was a good meeting but no real action taken. I did learn that the local folks eat with their hands, which is a challenge when you're having a fried egg. They graciously offered me a fork.

In the afternoon we visited a parcel of land that Ranjan would like to buy. The property will cost some US$35,000 and the demolition of the stately old house there another US$5,000. He figures he can put eight houses on the site, but our investment would be US$5,000 per unit before a single block is laid. I'm not too sure about this one. Later we stopped by Ranjan's son-in-law's place. He's the construction supervisor for Habitat here and we visited some about their work.

The next day, Sunday, we had breakfast at the house and then left for Kandy, an inland town some 130 Km from Moratuwa. We stopped for lunch at an elephant sanctuary at Pinnawala. We got there in time to watch the elephants leave the river and walk up the hill. They came within feet of us—very impressive. We drove on to Kandy, did some shopping, and checked into Earl's Regency Hotel, a very nice place that sits on a hillside overlooking the town. We then went to the

Kandy Cultural Center for a show of folk dance and music—an extravaganza that included fantastic costumes and fire-walking. That was a first for me.

That evening we visited a huge Buddhist temple compound, which is home to one of the poor old sage's teeth. It was an ordeal, actually. We had to take off our shoes at the entrance and then climb a gravel path to the temple itself. There was quite a line that moved slowly through the temple towards a window through which you could see the reliquary that holds the tooth. I guess. I can't say that I actually saw Buddha's tooth.

We left Kandy the next morning and drove into the countryside to visit a UCF preschool. We passed by a number of reservoirs that are part of an intricate and expansive irrigation system that was started 2,400 years ago. There are some 3,000 reservoirs in Sri Lanka and the engineering was unmatched in the West until the 19th century. We stopped at a wayside restaurant, but were told that all they had was fried rice. We were hungry so we said let's eat. As the honored westerner I was awarded with a fried egg on top of my fried rice. I was also allowed to use the sit-down toilet, once they found the key, rather than the squat toilet that they had for local folks. I was glad—my experiences with squat toilets have not been memorable. Well, memorable, maybe, but not happy. We passed many Buddhist shrines and a couple of Hindu temples along the way. Sri Lanka is a predominantly Buddhist country with Hindu and Christian minorities. The Tamil are Hindus and recent immigrants—they've only been on the island for some 300 years.

The next morning we visited the Habitat office and a couple of their houses—very nice actually. We went to another that was under construction—not so nice. Their program is now "Save and Build" requiring the beneficiary family to make a 12,000-rupee down payment before they start to build. They are then loaned 53,000 rupees to build with. This was to be a half-house with just a bedroom being built. Work had stopped, though, as the 65,000 rupees, about US$650, had been exhausted. $650 seems low for what they were planning to build—should be closer to $2,500. I can't seem to get this question answered. In the afternoon we had a fruitful discussion about costs generally and my concerns about the $35,000 lot they're looking at. I think that we're coming to terms. We went to a Chinese restaurant for dinner. I paid $21 for the five of us. I had "caramel' for dessert—turned out to be flan, but very good. I flew home uneventfully the next day.

EPILOGUE

This was my only trip to Sri Lanka. I'd like to go back some day. It's a beautiful country, a lot like India but without all of the people and noise. They've gone on to create a successful covenant partner there. They ended up not buying the US$35,000 parcel in Moratuwa. Instead they've focused on helping very poor people. They do a fair amount of rehab work and some new building and have done 126 projects since joining The Fuller Center. The Tamil uprising has been quelled. Interesting fact: the Tamil Tigers were the first to use suicide bombers to advance their cause. The Buddhists in the legislature have backed off on their efforts to prohibit Christian organizations from doing charitable work. They were losing believers due to the good works that the Christians were doing. Imagine that.

Ranjan comes to the States every year to raise funds for his various ministries and we generally get together. We were still living in Colorado for his first visit and that weekend we'd committed to help our son and his family move from Leadville to Dillon. Both cities sit higher than 9,000 feet above sea level and it's cold there more often than not. This was a cold weekend and I thought poor Ranjan might perish or never come to see us again. He survived and we have since moved to the more temperate clime of Americus, so we still see him regularly. He always brings us tea.

Sri Lanka represents what The Fuller Center stands for—grassroots organizations making decent housing a reality for God's people in need. I'm proud of what has developed since we first got together to dream about what might be done.

NICARAGUA

On September 26, 2006, we received a message on our website from a Danilo Gutierrez of Nicaragua. Danilo advised that he had previously been a part of Habitat's team but was no longer with them and asked about forming a Fuller Center there. At that time we were young and had commitments that we were finding hard to meet. We had operations in a half-dozen countries and were going through a bout of scarcity thinking. So we told Danilo that we couldn't start anything in Nicaragua yet but for him to stay in touch.

And stay in touch he did, writing regularly all through 2007, 2008, 2009, 2010. Finally, in late 2011 we relented, for a couple of reasons. One—he wore us out. And two—we realized that scarcity thinking didn't demonstrate much faith, and it was time for us to become abundance thinkers. So in early 2012 we signed a covenant with The Fuller Center Nicaragua, and what a blessing it turned out to be.

I think I've visited Nicaragua more than any of our other international sites. Ryan Iafigliola, our Director of International Field Operations (we don't pay much but we give really impressive titles) was the first of us to visit, going down in January of 2012. I didn't make my first trip until August of 2013 when I traveled there with our good friends Doug and Jill Miller and Doug's daughter Wendy. The Millers were on our first Global Builders trip to Nicaragua in early 2013 and fell in love with the place. We went down together to get the lay of the land and see what we might be able to do to have a lasting impact there.

Our work in Nicaragua began in the village of Las Peñitas, a half-hour east of León. Las Peñitas is a fishing village right on the Pacific coast. Its legal status is interesting. Much like an Indian reservation in the States, Las Peñitas sits on indigenous land, so part of the process of setting up shop there involved a visit to the tribal elders (who were delighted with the prospect of getting some decent housing up). It's a poor village. Most everyone is connected in some way to fishing, the rest to agriculture. The housing stock is abysmal. The newest houses were built a few years back by a misguided charitable operation that somehow missed Jesus' counsel to build on a solid foundation, so those houses are splitting in two. There's a lot of daub and wattle and a good number of plastic and tin structures. This is a place where we can make a significant difference.

In February of 2014 my friend David Forehand invited me to travel to Honduras to see some work that he'd been involved with along with some Methodist friends. They started working there after hurricane Mitch devastated the country in 1998. They called themselves the Heart of Georgia Christians in

Action (a name they considered modifying somewhat once they saw the acronym: HOG-CIA). We decided to have a stopover in Nicaragua since we were in the neighborhood. Our friends the Millers were there, on another Global Builders trip. Seems like the best way for me to see them is to travel to Nicaragua. Since David and I had failed to bring work clothes we weren't much help. Alas.

At its last meeting in 2014, the Fuller Center's Board of Directors decided that it needed to get a better feel for the work by traveling abroad. We chose Nicaragua, so in January of 2015 board members John Schaub, Allon Lefever, Bob Abel, Tamara Danel, Edgar Stoesz, and LeRoy Troyer along with my wife Sheilla and I and our Communications Director Chris Johnson hooked up with a Global Builders team and went to work. They divided us among four or five houses. Ours, owned by a man named Guillermo, needed work from the ground up, and from the ground I mean that literally. The soil in Las Peñitas could probably be mined for oil. It's black, has the consistency of cold tar, and is a major challenge to dig into. We prevailed and got the foundation dug and poured, the walls up and the roof on. We had the good fortune of having experienced hands like LeRoy and Edgar on our team who, despite being the elders of the group, worked their hearts out. Midway through the week Guillermo suffered a heart attack, so we didn't see him again. I did learn later that he had recovered and moved into the house.

On Saturday of that week we had our board meeting and it was a spiritual event. Having worked all week in this corner of the Lord's vineyard gave us all a special sense of the importance of what we are doing together.

We left for home the next day. Sheilla and I were both under the weather. I coughed so heartily on the trip from León to Managua that the board started discussing succession planning. Turns out I'd picked up bronchitis and Sheilla had the flu.

I made a quick trip in February of 2015 to meet up with—you guessed it—Doug Miller. This was another Global Builders trip led by Doug's daughter, Wendy. Doug asked me to join them so that we could spend a little more time on the ground talking through ways that we could help the local group. Wendy's husband Laurent was along. He's an accomplished metal-worker and spent the week building scaffolding—something most of our covenant partners anywhere would covet.

The year 2015 marked the 10th anniversary of The Fuller Center and we decided that the best way to celebrate was with a 10 house building project. We chose Nicaragua because we knew that they could get the job done and they certainly need the houses. Sheilla joined me on this trip along with her brother Doug Winkka, Chris Johnson, his wife, Shellie, Stacey Odom-Driggers Allen Slabaugh, and another 30 intrepid souls. I didn't keep good notes of this trip, but Sheilla did, so I'm sharing some of her observations.

One of the things I do at the Fuller Center is talk to many people who have gone on a Global Builders trip to see how the trip went for them and to find out if there are things we need to improve (other than the fact that there's generally not enough hot water, all goes extremely well). These trips are all out of the country. Helping a family build a simple, decent home in which to live is truly an unforgettable experience. The new houses are most often made of cinder blocks with cement floors—a real improvement over a dirt floor and plastic walls. I used to get weepy when I talked about this but not long ago I asked myself, why? I am helping a family really improve their life and I should be happy about what the Fuller Center is doing in the U.S. and around the world.

We flew down on Spirit Airlines—a first. We got the tickets through Airlink, an organization that helps nonprofits with travel. All we had to pay was the tax—$67 each—so we couldn't pass it up. Of course there were drawbacks—we got to Managua at 2:30 in the morning. But otherwise we were treated well—no baggage fees, priority boarding, and we sat in the first row.

We set off for Las Peñitas around 9:30 the next morning in a school bus—ninety degrees and no air conditioning but the windows opened part way, so we just pretended that it was a 1955 road trip. We stopped in León for sightseeing at the cathedral and did some grocery shopping. The cathedral is spectacular. They say that the plans for it were sent from Spain but somehow the León plans got switched with those for Lima, Peru, so the Lima cathedral is in León and León's is in Lima.

In Las Peñitas we settled into Hotel Suyapa where we had air conditioning, warmish water for showers (the water is stored in a huge tank on the roof and is heated by the sun) a flush toilet and internet. What more could you ask for? Well I'll tell you—the hotel sits right on the beach!

It was a great week. The work is hard and the sun is hot but the result makes it all worth it. Pretty much everything is done by hand including mixing cement on the ground the way it's been done for centuries, though we had the luxury of a gas-

powered mixer for doing the floors—a gift from prior work campers who noted a certain inefficiency in mixing cement by hand. In the dirt.

We had some excitement that week. The volcano Momotombo erupted—the first time in 110 years. We could hear the boom of the eruption and watch the smoke and ash. With eruptions come earthquakes and with earthquakes come tsunamis, so we were given an evacuation plan: go downstairs, turn left out of the hotel, turn right at the first street, and run. Fortunately, we didn't have to put the plan to the test.

We went back to Managua in air-conditioned luxury. Since our flight home didn't leave until 2:30 a.m. Sunday (Spirit Airlines), we had a day to kill in Managua, so we decided to go to the mall. There were seven of us so we took two taxis, four in one with Spanish-speaking David aboard, three in the other with no one speaking the language. We got to the mall to discover that the second cab wasn't behind us. Turns out the driver stopped for a bite to eat but his poor passengers had no idea where they were or where they were going and no way to ask. The mall was a big disappointment so we had the cabs take us to Salvador Allende Park, a newer tourist site on the banks of Lake Managua. We had a bite to eat but our shopping quest was unsatisfied. We ended up shopping at the tourist stalls at the airport.

My last trip to Nicaragua in March, 2016, was a fundraiser—the never-ending quest of a nonprofit. I met some old friends there, a father and son who were looking to make an investment in kindness, and did in a big way. We toured the building sites, met some of the families, and enjoyed being at the beach. I also met a representative of New Story Charity, the group that has made such a difference with us in El Salvador. We checked out a potential site for a new subdivision and looked like we might put something together. It turned out that the land is owned by the municipal government and they wanted an exorbitant price for it. Try as we might we couldn't seem to find their better nature to appeal to, so the deal fell through.

EPILOGUE

Nicaragua was a prime site for our work for many years. The Global Builders teams all had a great time there. The work was rewarding and the beach was lovely. But things have taken a bad turn and civil unrest has forced us to suspend our operations. Many of our leadership team served with the Sandinista forces during the civil war—some were recruited as young as 15. They all said that while they remained Sandinistas they were no longer Danielistas and looked forward to Ortega's departure from the government. Apparently they weren't alone, and today there is a major uprising against what's become dictatorial rule under Ortega and his wife. We pray for an early resolution to the crisis so that our work can continue there.

PERU

December, 2007

I'm once again at the Colorado Springs airport getting ready for a new adventure. I'm going to Peru, my first trip to South America. It's springtime there but fully winter in Colorado. It's hard to travel from a cold place to a warm one. You need to bundle up to get to the airport and those bundles become a burden for the rest of the trip. It will be a long day. From the Springs I go to Atlanta and then on to Lima—16 hours of travel.

I got to Lima at midnight. Our man on the ground there, Zenón Colque, picked me up and took me to the Sta. Maria Hotel on Avenida de la Marina. Zenón and I were born on the same day, and while he looks like he just came in from Machu Picchu and I look like a recent arrival from Britain, we call ourselves twin brothers. We'll head out to the countryside tomorrow.

We left Lima on a Soyuz bus at 11:00 heading for Cañete. There we went to the office of the *Sociedad de Beneficiencia Pública de Cañete* (the Public Charity Society) where we met with Zulma Matamay, Oscar Saavedra and Manuela Grimaldo, who are members of The Fuller Center steering committee. The Society is a clearing house for government and public assistance programs.

Cañete is on the northern edge of the area most damaged by the 2007 earthquake. There isn't a lot of visible damage here, although on the inside the Society's building looks like another tremor will bring it down. From there we went up the Pan-American Highway a ways and then over towards the coast and headed south. We traveled through a number of coastal villages—Playa Hermosa, Santa Cruz, Santa Barbara. Much of the initial clean-up has been done, leaving mile after mile of debris and broken dreams. Most of the more severely damaged houses were built of adobe, so the ridge of rubble will gradually melt into a seaside wall of dirt. The results of the quake are seen in neighborhood after neighborhood of international tents—white ones from USAID and Caritas, blue ones from the EU and the Peruvian government. They estimate that 25 thousand to 30 thousand houses were destroyed and countless others severely damaged.

We then turned inland and traveled through La Quebrada, San Benito, Imperial, old and new, and finally arrived at one of the eeriest places I've visited, the village of La Florida. The village sits at the edge of the Andean foothills. It could be on the far side of the moon. The town stops suddenly and at its edge is—nothing. The hillsides are devoid of vegetation. The earth is dark brown. There's no sand. There's just—nothing. For as far as you can see, unless you look back towards town. There's a small river running through it and the soil, despite its barren look, is fertile, so La Florida is like an oasis in this brown desert.

We left Cañete the next morning and travelled south to Chincha. We drove along the coastal desert—another stretch of desolation. We encountered a number of villages, mostly deserted, of small, square houses made out of *esteras*, woven mats, supported by bamboo pillars. It wasn't clear why these villages were built or who lived in them. They do give the area an unusual look.

The earthquake hit at 6:40 PM on August 15th with a force between 7.9 and 8.4 on the Richter scale. Even at the lower estimate it was a quake of significant force. The area most affected was between Cañete and Pisco. Thousands of unreinforced, adobe structures were destroyed and over 500 lives were lost. The area around Chincha was especially hard hit. In some areas building foundations settled 18-24 inches, up-heaving the interior floors. In Tambo de Mora I got permission to climb onto the roof of the severely damaged town hall to take pictures of the Plaza de Armas (the central plaza in Peruvian cities is called the Plaza de Armas—not sure why), which had been turned into a refugee camp. Most of the furnishings in the town hall had been cleared out. The second floor was a library and museum and still had a display with the remains of a pre-conquest Indian. I couldn't help but wonder how many earthquakes those bones had survived.

From Chincha we traveled by bus to Pisco, a larger city that was also severely damaged. Much of the debris has been cleaned up leaving mile after mile of mounds of adobe bricks. Housing for the newly homeless is in tents that bear the names of the benefactors, some coming from as far away as Turkey. There are a few more substantial wooden units that the Peruvian government is installing, but these are billed as temporary as well. Entire neighborhoods that were once adobe brick are now canvas.

The message is that there is plenty of work to be done. Our group in Cañete is prepared to help get The Fuller Center operating locally and Zenón is working to assemble what could become a national board. The site at La Florida offers hope. It would require a healthy investment in infrastructure though. Another option would be to work in the damaged neighborhoods, a block at a time. A challenge would be with repayments, as Zenón has had trouble in the past getting people to pay for improvements on their own land. These decisions will be made locally and Zenón has the experience to pull things together.

From Pisco we returned to Cañete to meet with the Bishop, a great guy and a solid complement to the team. The next day we met with representatives of the Diocese at the Instituto Juan Pablo II in the Lima suburb of Manchay, a relatively young settlement of migrants from the mountains. It reminds me of Matamoros in Tijuana. It's barren, as is most of coastal Peru, with a few paved streets and lots of dust. There is surprisingly little litter, which was true of most of the countryside we visited. Manchay is a shantytown and presents another opportunity for The Fuller Center. The Instituto, once completed, will be a huge benefit to the local population. They will offer courses in baking, cooking, sewing, arts & crafts, metalworking and cabinetry. They could be a significant partner in our work.

We then returned to Lima. I leave for home on the late flight. The Lima airport may be my favorite after Schiphol in Amsterdam. It's clean, modern and efficient and the shops don't close at 9:00, so we late-night fliers have something to do.

November, 2009

I'm back in Lima. Ryan Iafigliola, our Director of International Field Operations, is joining me on this trip—his first abroad. I came here from North Korea with a stopover in Atlanta. I started this trip in the Philippines, so it's been quite the jaunt. When I got to the airport there was no sign of Zenón. We got in at 1:15 AM, about a half-hour early, and I was among the first off the plane, sailed through passport and customs and, since I only brought a carry-on, didn't have to wait for a bag. I figured that since I was so early he just hadn't gotten there yet, so I wandered through the crowds, which were significant. After a half-hour I spotted Ryan. It turned out that they'd been there since Ryan's plane arrived about an hour before mine and were having a bowl of soup in the restaurant—never thought to look there. It's late now and I'm beginning to fade. I slept on the plane from Beijing and again on the flight from Atlanta, so I'm not sleep deprived. But my body thinks it's noontime and is a little confused by the darkness.

We're here to dedicate the first 20 houses. After all of our wandering on my last trip they've settled on La Florida—a good choice. Zenón is promising a gala event, something he's good at, and I'm sure it will be. Zenón is quite the mover and shaker. He's known Millard Fuller for years and headed up Habitat's work in Peru.

The next day started with errands, ordering Bibles and picking up a banner for the big event. I bought a Quechua Bible to add to my collection. We left Lima at 11:30 and took the Pan-American Highway to Cañete. We stopped for lunch at a

54

place called El Piloto and Zenón and I split an order of beef and *taku-taku*, a very tasty bean and rice patty. Then we headed into the hills for La Florida.

The place looked different to me, partly because there's now a paved road all the way into town. The Fuller Center houses stand out. Many of the houses there are made of *estera*, mats made of woven bamboo. Ours are solid brick, a vast improvement. 18 are all but done, another about 70% there, and the 20th is just a foundation due to a vacillating homeowner who can't decide between a free government house and one of ours. He won't make the cut.

After touring the village we took a ride through the mountains to the Cañete River Valley. It's a very fertile area full of farms. The road was a little bit like the Phantom Canyon between Victor and Cañon City in Colorado, without the guardrails. Or the trees. It was beautiful though, maybe more like the road to Trishuli in Nepal. We drove through the river bottom to check out a collection of Incan and pre-Incan ruins. We paid the guard to walk us through and saw the Inca's palace, the Temple of the Sun, the granary and the armory. The Temple originally had 60 pillars that marked the movement of the sun. The buildings were plastered with fool's gold so the clever Spanish scraped off the plaster in their search for riches. The buildings were built of stone with clay mortar. All along the highway were the remnants of Incan roads hugging the hillside. Along the way I was introduced to *cañihuaco*, a grain that they say is twice as nutritious as quinoa. Tomorrow we celebrate.

Up early today. Zenón made pancakes and Megan, the Peace Corps volunteer who's been helping out, is making macaroni and cheese for the pot luck. Her friend is making guacamole—the avocados are huge. We're staying at a house that Zenón rents and uses as a volunteer center. Ryan and I shared lodgings last night and I hear that my snoring kept him awake—could be a long day for him.

The event was scheduled to start at 11:30 so we left the house at 11:45. We went straight to the office in La Florida where I signed all of the Bibles. Then we ambled up the hill where four of the houses are clustered. There was an Andean band playing a *charango*, a lute-like instrument with at least 10 strings, a flute, a pan flute and drum. They were quite good. The event itself got started at about 1:00. There were lots of speeches, including mine. Towards the end of the speech making the president of Nuevo Imperial arrived. He had proclamations for Ryan and me and gave us caps and vests.

We then started touring the house sites, dedicating them as we went. The Catholic priest hadn't arrived yet so a couple of Protestant pastors blessed the houses. Interestingly, when the priest finally did show up the pastors quietly disappeared. We visited all 19 of the almost completed houses—they're scattered all over town so it took a while. All in all it was a lovely day—hot and dusty but worth it.

One interesting custom—each house had a bottle of champagne, or in some cases beer, hanging from the lintel of the front door and the final act of dedication was to break it. This was done by the godparent of the house and more than once I was chosen. Most of the bottles were in a plastic bag so it wasn't too messy. The first one I hit was not, however, and I got a champagne shower. Before we were done I smelled like a bar. By then we were out of time, so we missed the pot luck in order to get back to the house and pack. We had dinner at El Piloto and I slept my way back to Lima. I managed to get a VIP pass at the airport so I spent my last few hours in Peru in luxury. I'm looking forward to being home—I need a break.

August, 2012

We're heading back to Peru. Sheilla is with me on this trip where we will actually build a house as a part of the Millard Fuller Legacy Build. We're going to build 10 houses in La Florida. The houses are started, so we'll be finishing them up. There are 40 of us—a relatively small group so we'll have to work extra hard. I'm looking forward to this as a getaway and it's especially nice to have Sheilla with me. It will be good to be out of Americus and away from the day-to-day worries. This work is an ongoing instruction in the principle of faith. I must be a slow learner.

The first full build day was great. We kicked things off yesterday with two events—a public welcoming ceremony by the local officials and another by the folks in La Florida. The public ceremony was a big deal. The mayor of Nuevo Imperial and the governor of La Cañete were there along with a dozen other dignitaries. We all walked around the plaza carrying a huge Peruvian flag. I was invited to raise the Nuevo Imperial flag and the governor and I raised the national flag. Three little girls then sang the national anthem and we all gave speeches. It was quite the event.

We were put up in a strange little hotel in Nuevo Imperial. It was a little tawdry and the owner forgot to turn the pump on to fill the roof tank, so we couldn't shower every day. The strangest feature was that there was no toilet seat. We didn't have to squat but we did have to hover. The trip between Nuevo Imperial and the house site was rich with agriculture. There were vast fields of sugar snap peas, which put a smile on Sheilla's face—she's a fan. There was also a field of artichokes. I wasn't sure what I was seeing so I asked the farmer. He wasn't sure either. He said he thought it was something they like to eat in America.

The work week went well. The walls were up so our job was to finish them. We're on house number 10, which will belong to Pastor Juan Lopez and his wife Kelly Joana. They have a small church right next to the house, so this will be convenient for them. House 10 is the farthest one out—pretty much near the end of the universe. We got the roof on, the floors poured and the interior partitions up, so the house was pretty much done by the time we left. Our house leader, long-time Fuller Center friend Peter Salemme, always likes to put a personal touch on the houses he builds. He chose a skylight for this one, so much to our concern he ended the week cutting a hole in the roof. I'm sure that the local folks will figure out how to plug it. Otherwise the house will be well ventilated. It was a great week—lots of old friends coming together to get some houses built.

EPILOGUE

I haven't been back to Peru since the Legacy Build in 2012, but the work there continues unabated. There are now 91 families living in decent homes in La Florida. Zenón continues to lead the effort despite "advancing" age. (Zenón and I were born on the same day and see ourselves as twins. He says that any difference in our appearance is due to the fact the he was given coffee as a baby and I was given milk.) La Florida is a testament to what one determined man and an army of volunteers can accomplish.

DAVID SNELL

ARMENIA

May Day 2008

It's May Day and there's no better place to celebrate the holiday than in a former Soviet Socialist Republic. I find myself in Yerevan, Armenia. It was a quiet day here—little traffic, stores closed. I went into the country to visit some building sites. It's Thursday evening and I got here Monday night. I didn't bring a notebook with me and for some reason I always have a little difficulty explaining to my hosts what I want and why. So I struck off on my own last night and found a journal to keep some notes in—its cover is a picture of Mount Ararat.

I had a great flight schedule for this trip. I left home at 1:15 for Atlanta, had a three-hour layover, and then took the overnight Air France flight to Paris. Another three-hour layover and then on to Yerevan, getting here at 9:00 pm local time. When I got off the plane there was a young man holding a sign with my name on it. I vainly thought it was my reception committee but, alas, it was an Air France worker who'd been sent to tell me that only one of my two bags had made the trip. I held my breath through passport control, wondering which of the two had come with me. I was greatly relieved when I got to the carousels and found that it was the big one. Most of my clothes, toiletries and electronics were on the ground. What I was missing was my underwear, extra shoes and my travel book and map. I would survive the inconvenience despite the fact that the next Air France flight wouldn't arrive until Wednesday night and the bag wouldn't be delivered until Thursday. It did and all was well.

Gohar, one of the Habitat leaders, met me at the airport and brought me into town to the Shirak Hotel. It's not bad by my typical international travel standards—it's pretty fancy, actually. I have a tiny balcony and a great view of Mt. Ararat. We headed out at about 10:00 PM to find a bite to eat, but failed in our effort to find an open café. We did find a mini-supermarket and I had my first your-not-in-Kansas-anymore experience. The store sold bread, cold cuts, cheese and dairy products, sodas and snacks, each at a separate stall. At each stall sat a woman—apparently the proprietress—and each stall had its own cash register. It was like being in a food mall. We bought some lavash—Armenian bread—some cheese, a soda, juice and a bottle of water. We paid separately for each. We were going to buy some cold cuts but the shopkeeper was closing and not about to make another sale. The storied Soviet style of customer service is apparently alive and well in some corners of the former empire.

The next day we'd arranged for Gohar to pick me up at 9:30, so I slept in. I had breakfast at the hotel—it's complimentary and not bad except for the instant coffee, the funny tasting cereal and the bizarre side dishes. Well, the eggs weren't bad.

We went to the Habitat office for a get-to-know-you meeting. It looks like there's no room for reconciliation with Habitat; they're just waiting to see how difficult they will be about the assets. We'll promote our relationship with no mention of Habitat. They've assigned some of their staff to the Fuller Center. The others are being paid from house payments, which amount to some $12,000 a month. They've built a dynamic program here and I don't understand why Habitat is willing to give it up.

We left at 1:00 for lunch and to do some underwear shopping. It was the tiniest bit awkward to be choosing my dainties in the company of folks I'd just met and hope to have a professional relationship with. The department store was a little like the supermarket—more of a bazaar with lots of small stalls. The first underwear lady decided that she didn't have anything that would fit me and was a little highhanded about it. The second lady, who only sold men's underwear and socks, found me a nice pair of boxers and two pairs of socks. I think I'll make it until my small bag arrives.

We went to the 'My Village' restaurant for lunch and spent an amazing amount of time discussing the menu. We decided to order family style, but apparently the choices were manifold and difficult. I was a mere observer as all of the discussion was in Armenian and my acquaintance with Armenian cuisine was in its infancy. We settled on barbeque but apparently couldn't decide between beef, pork or lamb, so we ordered all three. We also ordered salads and appetizers—not bad except for the cheese, which was a little heavy for my taste, and the yogurt soup which was, well, yogurt. The meat was excellent.

There's a young couple here, Kalen and Joelle, from Fresno. He's a contractor and wants to build a model village up north. They're both of Armenian descent and want to do something for the motherland. They invited me over to dinner. They're living here in Yerevan until they get their place built in the village. They have three little cuties—Judy, Peter and Frankie. I was able to do some emailing at their place. Then Kalen let me drive their Neva—an amazing Russian jeep—part of the way home. Very cool. I don't know if the future will see our projects intersecting—it would be great if they could.

Armenia is like a museum of old and some new Russian cars. Every other one is a Lada and those that aren't are Volgas. Most of the mini-buses and trucks are

Russian as well. There are more Russian cars here, 17 years after independence, than I remember seeing in Hungary, just five years after the fall. This is great stuff for a car buff like unto me.

The next morning we traveled north, into the countryside. We took the M4—a good four-lane highway—to Sevan, where we stopped to visit the 9th century church. It sits on a promontory overlooking the lake. The steps alone would dissuade a faint-hearted invader. It's like most of the old churches I've seen here—more vertical than horizontal. The interior space is relatively small in square footage but soars. We visited with a man selling candles and books. He's a coin collector and has most of the U.S. quarters. I had a couple but they were in the car at the bottom of the killer steps so I didn't offer them.

From Sevan we went through the mountains towards Vanadzor. We went through a tunnel dug under one of the mountains. The landscape changed dramatically from one end of the tunnel to the other. The south side was relatively dry and the north end opens to lush greenery. The woods are deciduous, but if they were pine it would look a lot like Colorado.

In Vanadzor we went to the Habitat office and met with their staff. We also visited a renovated apartment building and a half-built house. There are a lot of both here. Many of the Soviet era apartment houses weren't all that well built and are falling into disrepair while issues of ownership continue to be a challenge. There are also many half-houses here, houses that a family has started to build but hasn't had the money to complete.

Lunch was unique. The restaurant, which seemed pretty new, was a collection of private dining rooms. Ours was outfitted with a sofa and chairs, a private terrace, and a dining table that could seat a dozen. The first course was salads and vegetables, yogurt curd, some sort of slaw, tomatoes, cucumbers, green onions, cilantro, olives and hot green peppers. Then came the meat—barbequed lamb, pork and beef, served with lavash. The idea is to make a burrito with the lavash. They also served what they call lemonade but it didn't seem to have lemons in it and tasted a little like cough syrup. After lunch we headed back to Yerevan.

The next day we traveled to the southeast, to a place called Khor Virap. This is a farming village where Habitat has done a number of half-built homes. We visited with several families including three named Sargsyan. These are houses built over basements that the homeowners have started but can't complete. Calling them basements is generous—they're more like cellars with earth floors and dank, dark walls. There are other families who have been living in *domiks*. These are like shipping containers and were brought in by the hundreds after the 1988 earthquake. They were meant to be temporary housing but as too often is the case they became permanent and less hospitable with each passing year.

The houses are large by our international standards and quite nice. They're built of stone with tin roofs and plastered interior walls. The exterior walls are a little over a foot wide and made of two parallel runs of 5-inch block with a cement slurry poured between the two. This is to satisfy seismic code requirements. They top the structure with a cement slab ceiling over which they build a peaked roof with wooden trusses. The concrete ceiling seems like overkill to me. Interior partitions are made of a single run of 6-inch block except for the bearing wall which is a foot wide. The houses include a plumbed kitchen and bath with an on-demand water heater. The floors are polished concrete and the kitchen and bath walls are tiled. The street side of the exterior is plastered and the other three walls left raw. This makes for a lovely home. The families pay no more than US$10,000 for the finished house. By using half-builts they keep construction costs low and have no land or infrastructure costs.

One of the homeowners was making lavash so we were able to watch—it's a fascinating, cooperative undertaking involving three women with unique tasks. The dough, made of flour, salt, water and yeast, is made the night before and rolled into balls. The first woman rolls the dough onto a wooden disk about 12 inches wide and passes it to the second woman who rolls it out more on an oblong-shaped board about a yard long. She then passes it to the baker who lays it on a cushioned board of about the same size, dabs it with water in what looks to be the four points of a cross and then slaps it against the wall of the oven, vertically, where it quickly bakes. The oven is a round, well like pit, maybe two feet wide and two yards deep with a fire smoldering in the bottom. The fire heats the sides of the oven against which the bread is slapped and baked. She then uses an iron poker to pull the bread off the wall and sets it aside to cool.

We then went to the Khor Virap monastery, which is on a hill within sight of the Turkish border and Mt. Ararat. This is the site of the pit in which St. Gregory the Illuminator was held prisoner by King Trad for thirteen years. He was kept alive by local Christians who would drop food and water to him. King Trad went insane and somehow the saint was released whereupon he cured the king of his illness. In gratitude the king declared Armenia to be a Christian state—the world's first. This happened in 301, so I was standing in a place of continuous veneration for over 1700 years.

We then went to the home of Serap Sangsyan, where a number of homeowners had gathered to fix us lunch. They barbequed over a small fire in the yard. Part way through the meal they brought out the vodka and started toasting. I took four shots and then pleaded weakness. It was quite the bonding experience. After lunch we watched a video of the Catholicos Build. I was one with the people, a satisfying experience.

We left then for Yerevan and stopped along the way at Echmiadzin, the ecclesiastical center of the Armenia Apostolic Church. It's a large complex of offices, monasteries and the residence of the Catholicos. It's dominated by the cathedral. The site dates from the 301 establishment of the church. I don't know when the cathedral was first built but it was renovated in 484 and again in the 6th century, so it's plenty old. Armenia is a country that's been overrun and occupied repeatedly throughout its history but has managed to retain its separate identity. I think that the church has played a big role in that.

We got back to Yerevan at about 5:00. I wanted to check email and was told that they had wifi in the lobby of the Congress Hotel. Turned out I couldn't connect but the doorman told me that there was an internet café at the Moscow Cinema. He gave me a map and I headed off through Republic Square but I got misguided by a view of the opera house, which I thought was the Moscow Cinema, so ended up walking blocks out of my way. I finally found the place and was able to connect. The world seems smaller when you can check your email thousands of miles away from home.

The next morning we traveled to Yeghegnaszor to the east. The trip takes us past Khor Virap, through Ararat to Yeraskh, right on the closed border with Nakhchivan, Azerbaijan. From there we turned northeast and over the pass into Vets Door Region. We stopped at the Noravank Monastery, located about five miles up a steep gorge. About halfway up is a green park with picnic tables and a manmade waterfall—a gift to the country from a wealthy ex-pat. There are two renovated chapels dating from the 12th and 13th centuries. The lower level of the larger one is cellar-like, dark with a dirt floor. Flanking the front door are two staircases cantilevered from the wall to form a peak over the lower door. The steps are frighteningly narrow and provide access to the upper chapel, which is light, airy and domed—the hardest to get into and the loveliest to be in.

From there we traveled to Yeghegnadzor. We went to the Habitat office, where we had coffee, and then on to visit some homes. In the Grigorian house there was a piano—something you don't often see in our houses. Their daughter Armene played us a tune. We visited another Grigorian family and encountered what looked like a long pizza oven but was actually a lavash baker. Mrs. Grigorian had just made bread which was stacked high on the kitchen table. She and a friend get together every couple of weeks to bake bread. We then visited the Janians. This was the second place I visited that had a cow from Heifer International. He also had some homemade vodka, so we had to share a toast. Fiery.

We had lunch at a roadside restaurant that also featured private dining rooms. Same basic meal, but barbequed fish this time. From there we went to Areni where a number of houses have been built. There's a winery there and we got the VIP tour. We tasted a couple—a very light white and a semi-sweet red. I got a gift of each—hope they make it home. We got back to Yerevan in time for me to check email at the Moscow Cinema and watch the fountain in Republic Square. It dances with the music that comes from the National Museum.

The next day was a restful one. It poured rain all morning which kept us inside. In the afternoon we went to the Vernissage craft market to look for souvenirs. We ate at a place called Lahmadjo probably because all they serve is *lahmadjo*, a tortilla like thing made of a ten-inch round piece of lavash covered with a meat paste and folded over—very tasty. They serve it with *tan*, a buttermilk-like drink made of yogurt. The free time gave me a chance to make some notes about this ancient land:

Armenia is a country of emigrants. If all those who claim its heritage lived here it would be fairly densely populated. As it is, only about 25% of the world's Armenians live in Armenia. It's a country at the crossroads of history but has seldom been as independent as it is today. Until 1991 it was a Soviet Socialist Republic, and even today there are more Ladas on the roads than Toyotas.

This is an ancient place, and one that has a long history with Christianity. It is believed that two apostles, Saints Thaddeus and Bartholomew, brought the faith here early in the 1st century. It was the first country to adopt Christianity as the state religion—in 301, well before Constantine—when the grateful king was cured of insanity by St. Gregory after keeping the saint in a pit for 13 years.

Armenia is a country that defies categorization. It's located in Asia, but is distinctly European. It is a Christian country that is struggling to recover its spiritual roots after suffering 70 years of Soviet state atheism. Its overall economic condition places it among the developed nations, but it has significant pockets of third world living standards.

Present-day Armenia is defined in part by a tremendously destructive earthquake that struck the nation in 1988. In response to the devastating loss of housing, metal shipping containers called domiks *were brought in from across the Soviet Union to provide temporary shelter. Today, three decades after the disaster, thousands of families find themselves permanently housed in these boxes, which long ago outlived themselves. I'm here to sign the Partnership Covenant with The Fuller Center Armenia, a dedicated group who embrace our basic principles and have a sincere desire to eliminate poverty housing in this faraway place. They were a Habitat for Humanity affiliate until recently when they fell out of favor due to their refusal to use interest-bearing mortgages and lost access to the volunteer program, which was a vital part of their revenue. A focus of The Fuller Center Armenia will be to help families move from domiks into simple, decent homes. The traditional building material here is stone, which is expensive and difficult for volunteers to work with, so efforts are underway to develop new building technologies so that donor funds can build more houses.*

Armenia is an ancient country, and has been Christian for a long, long time. I've stood in churches that were built in the fourth, fourteenth, and seventeenth centuries. There's something profound about lighting a candle in a place where people have been praying for sixteen hundred years. But Armenia's spiritual history predates Christianity. Southwestern Armenia lies in the shadow of Mount Ararat, where Noah and his Ark are said to have settled when the flood waters abated. The father of Armenia, Hayk Nahapet, is said to have been a direct descendant of Noah.

The founders of The Fuller Center Armenia have been helping families have decent homes for a number of years and have developed unique approaches that allow them to build in the face of high land and materials costs and demanding building codes. Much of the work they've done has been in completing homes that families have started but not had the resources to finish. I've had the good fortune of meeting many of these families and visiting their homes. I've been served so much coffee that I may never sleep again (Armenian coffee is stout, and has the consistency of syrup). I've been treated with an in-home piano concert and been toasted with vodka—both Russian and home-brewed—and local wine (it comes in recycled soda bottles), and made to feel a welcome guest everywhere I've been. And all this despite the embarrassing fact that I've had to carry a cheat sheet to remember how to say good day (barev tzez) *and goodbye* (hadjo).

July 2016

I'm back in Armenia. Sheilla is with me this time along with Ryan Iafigliola. We're here with a Global Builders team for the 2016 Millard Fuller Legacy Build. The plan is to finish the work on a 16-unit condominium-style building. All of the homeowners are moving out of *domiks,* the shipping containers that were brought in from the Soviet Union after the 1988 earthquake. Some have been living in these metal crates for 27 years, so having a new, decent home will be a true blessing.

We started the week in Yerevan. We were there on a Sunday and went to church at St. Gregory the Illuminator Cathedral. It was an impressive service; most of it except for the sermon was chanted. We didn't understand a word of it, but it was quite something. We then traveled to the work site in Vanadzor, a town of some 82,000 people. Its economy has declined since independence and its population along with it from a high of some 150,000. Part of the town is dominated by a huge Soviet-era chemical plant that's abandoned and fallen into disrepair. Aside from that it's a lovely spot

We're staying at the Hotel Argishti. Sheilla and I were given a suite—we've got a living room with huge, overstuffed furniture, a dining table and refrigerator. The side walls of the bathtub are so tall that you take your life in your hands getting out of it. Otherwise it's great and we're feeling pretty special.

We're working on a four-story building with four units on each floor. The building was pretty much done. Our job was to paint and do finish work. It was a messy job. I'm always amazed on these projects at how few people know how to use a paintbrush. We got the job done. I spent most of Friday cleaning paint off the door jambs. Frustrating work.

On Friday afternoon the families started arriving, all carrying a small table and a basket of food. The tables were set in the living rooms and laden with bread, salt, wine, fruit and chocolates. An Orthodox priest visited each unit and blessed it and then the toasts began. A number of the families brought cognac, and I was obliged to have a sip or two. By the end of the visits I was in a jolly mood.

We then got ready to load up for the trip back to Yerevan. A man pulled up in an old Lada with the passenger seat replaced by a cotton candy machine. I hadn't seen one of those since my childhood, so naturally I had to have some.

EPILOGUE

With able leadership on the ground and significant support from the Armenian diaspora community in the United States, Armenia has become our most productive covenant partner with over 650 families housed since 2008. I was there with my wife Sheilla in June of 2018 to celebrate their 10th anniversary as a Fuller Center organization. It was a great trip—we got to help pour the floor in a new home alongside a Global Builders team; we met the Catholicos of All Armenians, the head of the Armenian Apostolic Church; and celebrated the 10th anniversary in grand style. The Fuller Center Armenia continues to set a high standard for covenant partners around the world.

DAVID SNELL

HAITI

Summer, 2010

When we first announced our Haiti initiative following the devastating January 2010 earthquake our long-time friend and counselor Edgar Stoesz wrote to urge caution. Edgar has a long history with Haiti and knows firsthand the challenges of working there. He counseled us to move deliberately, to engage local partners carefully, to assure that Haitians were at the forefront of the effort, and, above all, to be patient. As we had no prior experience in Haiti we listened carefully to Edgar's advice. This was a little frustrating to some of our supporters, who were anxious, as we were, to get houses built. But it paid off and we are now on the ground, allowing us to work with solid partners and get construction underway.

By August we'd had two work teams travel to Haiti—brave souls who were willing to test the system. The first, from Indianapolis, raised the first duplex at Saintard, to the northwest of Port-au-Prince, and helped lay the foundation for a second. A group from the Alfred Street Baptist Church in Alexandria, VA, traveled to Léogâne to begin in-fill work on a house there. ASBC has a relationship with the Lott Carey missionary alliance, one of our partners in Léogâne.

The Chronicle of Philanthropy reports that U.S.-based relief agencies received $1.3 billion in donations for Haiti relief, a remarkable sum. Some of that money went to immediate relief efforts—food, medicine, temporary shelter. To date little has gone into permanent housing, which is our mission. The earthquake took 230,000 lives and destroyed 250,000 homes. Estimates are that some 1.6 million people were left living in tents and makeshift shelters.

The Fuller Center is eager to do its part. We surely won't solve the entire problem, but we will help lead the way. Our approach is to build simple, decent houses that are earthquake, hurricane and fire resistant, houses that provide a clean and safe place for families to make homes in. The houses will be small by American standards, and pretty basic, but for a family that has been living in a pup tent for six months they will be little palaces.

October, 2010

I was up at 4:00AM to catch a 6:30 flight to Miami, then on to Haiti. I got to Port-au-Prince at 10:30, flew through passport control, and was met by the folks from the Notre Dame facility in Léogâne who will be my hosts for the next couple of days. There's evidence of the earthquake all the way from the airport to Léogâne, but not the terrible devastation that I expected. Much of the rubble has been cleared and the roads are passable but not good. It's hard to tell how much is quake damage and how much is just poor infrastructure driven by poverty.

Port-au-Prince reminds me a little of Kinshasa—the same grinding poverty and decrepit infrastructure. The best evidence of the earthquake is in the tent cities, which are everywhere and speak to the need for our being here. They're filled with people who don't seem to have anything to do. This is not a boot-strapping kind of place. From what I've read and seen this is a country that's been severely damaged by charity. It isn't universal, though. Yves, one of our homeowners put in so many volunteer hours that he's become part of the staff.

We met up with a young American-Haitian couple, Heather and Gerson, who have been doing some work in Léogâne. She's from the States, he's Haitian. They met and married a few years back and started a small development nonprofit—Building Hope for Haiti. They were about to set it aside when the earthquake hit and decided to spend a few months with the recovery effort. They had access to land and we teamed up with them to build some houses. It's been a good partnership. They both speak Creole, which solves the language problem, and they have an SUV, so we have wheels.

We visited the first Lott Carey house, an overlarge structure that was designed to fit the slab that the pre-quake house sat on. The thought was that having the slab in place would balance the extra cost of the larger house. It turned out that the slab was bad and had to be replaced, so the house ended up costing $7,500 and the owners still aren't satisfied. We then visited a couple of the houses using the new $4,500 plan—they're quite nice. We'd started the trip at Heather and Gerson's land, to which they now have clear title and on which our containers are sitting. They're loaded with two buildings worth of a Styrofoam block building system, which have cost us a fortune to ship, get out of customs and transport overland. One is supposed to be a house, the other a clinic.

The containers are a sorry sight. They brought two cranes in to move them off their trailers. One couldn't lift them and the other got stuck in the mud. A third showed up but wouldn't even enter the site unless we built a road. So we're building a little road so that we can get the containers on the ground. These will be the most expensive units we put up in Haiti—and they were free! Oh yeah, to further brighten the matter our guy on the ground gave one of the units to the Episcopal Church in exchange for their customs waiver. So the remaining four-plex is all we're left with and will end up costing us—I don't even know, but a bundle.

We went to the beach—very nice. There was a restaurant run by a French couple serving very good, if somewhat pricey, French fare. I had the *poissons grille* and it was worth the trip. We then went to look at the houses being built by the Cooperative Baptist Fellowship. I was intrigued by the concept, which is basically to erect a hollow, steel mesh-wall, which is then filled with rubble, of which there is an abundance in Haiti right now. Unfortunately, the execution is weak. In one unit the interior wall was visibly out of plumb and in another the door and window openings were not square front to back. They looked slapdash and if we're going to use the system some improvement will be needed.

After dinner I went up to the rooftop of the dormitory building to commune with the moon. This is a facility run by Notre Dame University to house some of their people who are working on public health issues as well as the occasional work team and folks like me. They gave me the presidential suite—I have A/C and hot water! There's a field behind the building and, like hundreds of such fields between here and Port-au-Prince, it's filled with tents. I don't know how many, but there must be a couple hundred in this field alone. I sat there in the moonlight on the roof of my safe and comfortable lodgings, and looked out over the sea of displaced humanity. There are hardly any lights. If I didn't know that it was a field of tents it would be hard to tell what it was. The place was quiet—almost silent—except for the giggling of little kids. Lots of giggling—how sweet that they're all too young to realize how dire their situation is.

Gerson and I talked a lot about the social dynamics of this place. He was raised in Darfour, just up the road, but got his higher education in the States. He's very clear about what's wrong with Haiti. He's as unsure as any of us about how to fix it. Haiti is a country whose social fabric has been severely damaged by kindness. I've been told that there were 10,000 nonprofits at work here before the earthquake. That number has surely risen.

The unintended result of years of international largesse is a country that no longer knows how to take care of itself, one that feels entitled to continuing support without having to work for it. This plays havoc with our self-help model and makes any sort of repayment program a challenge. A couple of Gerson's points were very interesting. Haitians have heard the talk of the quake providing the opportunity to build a better Haiti, and they like the idea of starting with bigger and better homes. Haitians know that millions of dollars were raised for earthquake relief and they feel that it's their money and they want it now. History and experience have made Haitians leery of the future and so they are willing to take a lesser benefit today rather than a greater one tomorrow. Many would rather have a free temporary house now than wait—and have to work for—a permanent house down the line.

The next day began with a meeting with Pastor Saul, a thoroughly disagreeable man who seems to typify the entitlement mentality that's so debilitating to this place. He's the head of the Lott Carey church, one of our funding partners, and he told me how unprincipled we are for imposing sweat equity requirements on his poor people. A gift, after all, is a gift and shouldn't be sullied by conditions. I went through our whole dignity and self-worth arguments and thought I was making headway only to end up at the same place. We ended it with our agreeing to put our positions in a letter. He's going to write his first and then I'll respond. (I never did get that letter.)

Mike Bonderer picked me up at about 10:30 in his brand new Mahindra pickup—a gift from the Knights of Malta. We stopped by Yves' house in Léogâne and took off for Port-au-Prince. By 2:00 we'd made it to the Catholic Relief Service office. It looks like they're going to help move Mike's wall forms through customs, so it was a successful meeting. Mike works with us in El Salvador and has a poured wall system that we've used on some of the houses there. He's added Haiti to his work load.

We finally got to the hotel at about 6:00—we were pretty much in traffic for five of the seven hours since we left Léogâne. The hotel is like an oasis from the noise and bleakness of Port-au-Prince. It's a complex of small buildings laid out in a garden of green. The place is called Villa MaMika and is in Croix-des-Bouquets. Mike and I spent the evening talking philosophy and making plans. We're ready to hit the ground running tomorrow. There's a group here of young people from the States and Spain who are with Clowns without Borders. You can't make this stuff up.

We started the next day with the Jesuits. They have a large parcel where they're putting in a trade school. They made space there for other NGOs including a group called Techo de Mi Pais out of Chile that's building temporary plywood houses and another called Rescue 911 made up of first responders from New York City. The Jesuits are building classrooms for their school as well as small, portable schools that can be taken out to the tent camps.

From there we traveled out to Balan, which is just east of a town called Ganthier. Balan is a collection of communities near the shores of a lake called Étang

Saumâtre, which means brackish pond. It's a poor place. The people are goatherds, and much of the housing is daub and wattle with thatch roofs. The houses are spread out over a large area, but instead of jungle the flora is scrub. It reminds me a little of Arizona. The Jesuits have built an elementary school and are working on a high school. They built a convent for some nuns who ended up not coming. It would make a great volunteer center if we were to build here. Another solid feature of the site is a water project that is bringing fresh water from a spring some four kilometers away with spigot stands throughout the village.

I just got back from Haiti. It was my first trip down there and it was an eye-opener. I didn't want to go just after the quake—the Fuller Center for Housing isn't a disaster relief organization and I figured I'd just be in the way. My plan was to wait and go down when I could dedicate the first batch of houses that we, naively as it turns out, thought we'd get built right away. But like many of our donors I was getting increasingly curious about the slow pace of things.

The Fuller Center is at work in some pretty challenging places around the world, but Haiti sets a new standard. We've managed to get ten houses built, six in Léogâne and another four in Saintard. It turns out that the Fuller Center is one of the very few groups that has managed to get any permanent housing built at all, so while I wish the numbers were higher they're actually pretty good.

There is some temporary housing getting built, but not much. We decided early on that we wouldn't go that route, primarily because too often temporary housing ends up becoming a permanent slum. We've seen temporary housing outlive itself by many years in places like Armenia, Peru and even here on the Pine Ridge Indian Reservation. Ironically, much of the temporary housing costs nearly as much as the permanent structures we're putting up and, in Haiti, even the temporary housing just isn't going up that fast.

There are a number of reasons that things are moving so slowly. One clear issue is land—apparently everyone is having the same difficulty we've found in finding affordable land to build on. Many, probably most, of the people living in tents today were in rented houses before the quake, which limits the in-fill potential for groups like ours. We don't want to build for a landlord with no control over the rents that could be charged. We finally have land with clear title in Léogâne where we'll be able to build 30 to 50 houses. The first foundations are going in there, so we are in motion.

Other challenges are more social than physical. In Mexico they used to say, "Poor Mexico, so far from God, so close to the United States." This is sadly the case for Haiti as well. In many ways this is a country that has been destroyed by kindness. The unintended consequence of this has been to rob many in Haiti of the dignity they deserve and to create attitudes of entitlement. Our model here at the Fuller Center seeks to restore dignity and to engage the beneficiaries in their futures. This is harder to do when so many feel that having a permanent house is more of a right than a blessing.

What I brought back from Haiti is that in the face of great tragedy there is a spark of hope. We won't solve the housing crisis there on our own, but we will help as many families as we can to have a simple, decent place to live.

January, 2011

It's been a year now since disaster struck Haiti, bringing additional tragedy to an already broken country. The public response to the earthquake was phenomenal, with millions of dollars raised and thousands volunteering to help relieve the suffering. Unfortunately, relief has been slow in coming and today over a million people continue to live in tent camps. Cholera has struck down thousands, and civil unrest has further slowed progress.

Haiti was a tough country to work in when times were good. The lack of a secure land title system has greatly slowed the rebuilding effort as donor agencies are understandably reluctant to have their investments go astray. The weak infrastructure, poor roads, and onerous customs regulations make it difficult to get things into the country and then to move them from place to place.

There is hope, though, for Haiti's future by looking to the country's past. In the 1700's Haiti was the richest of the French possessions. It was the first Latin American colony to claim independence and the first black-led republic in the world. Haitian troops served admirably alongside American Revolutionaries and with Simón Bolivar in South America's wars for independence. Upwards of 10,000 Haitian refugees settled in New Orleans in the early 1800s and helped shape south Louisiana's unique language and traditions. Jean Baptiste Point de Sable, one of the founders of what is now Chicago, and John James Audubon were born in Haiti.

One of the lessons that should come out of Haiti is that charity is a fragile commodity, one that needs to be handled with care. Reports are that before the earthquake there were over 10,000 nonprofits working there, all with the best intentions, but too often with unintended results. There is no denying that the people of Haiti have suffered unimaginable struggles. There is also no denying that Haiti has become a recipient nation, relying too much on the goodwill of others at the expense of its own sense of self-worth. The looming question, then, is how can we reach out and help our fellow human beings in need without creating an unhealthy dependency? At The Fuller Center for Housing, we believe we have a model that works—a hand-up, not a hand-out approach that requires that our partner families participate in the construction of their homes and pay the costs, on terms they can afford, over time with no interest charged or profit made. This goes a long way toward insuring that dignity is retained and self-reliance is built.

Fixing Haiti is a huge undertaking, one that involves more than just repairing the physical damage. Haiti's future depends on the ability of its people to become engaged in their country's success. It will require that donors do more than simply give *things*, but that they find ways to give *dignity*. The Fuller Center seeks to be a model in that, rebuilding hope one house at a time.

EPILOGUE

In 2011 we began working with a Haitian Christian ministry called Grace International to build houses on land they own in Lambi. The project was a great success and engaged many volunteers who became loyal supporters of the work there. In October, 2014, I traveled to Haiti to join in the celebration to dedicate the 56 houses built there. It was a short but joyful trip.

Good fortune, or what I like to call a Providential Confluence, introduced us to some new friends in a place called Pignon, a village in the north some 80 miles (and 5 hours) south of Cap Haïtien. Our leader there, Geral Joseph, has done a remarkable job of putting the organization together. They're building a very attractive home at a modest cost and recently completed the first house in Haiti paid for entirely from homeowner's payments—a great event anywhere but especially so in Haiti, where they said it couldn't be done. So far over 210 Haitian families have a decent place to call home thanks to our generous donors and volunteers.

DAVID SNELL

THE CONGOS

In 2007 we got a proposal to look into projects in The Republic of the Congo and the Democratic Republic of the Congo (formerly Zaire) from Jim Conway, who ran the World Food Program there and was connected to USAID. This led to a fascinating trip to both countries. The Republic of the Congo is the smaller of the two and was, until 1960, a French colony. Its capital, Brazzaville, lies just across the Congo River from Kinshasa, the capital of the Democratic Republic of the Congo (DRC), a former Belgian colony. Both countries are French speaking with a number of local languages and dialects.

July 2007

I left on Independence Day and arrived in Kinshasa on the 5th. I was met by a representative of USAID and got the VIP treatment. Jim Conway and Pierre Maloka met me in the lounge. Pierre is from the Equator Province and knew Millard and Linda when they were in Mbandaka in the early 1970s. He's currently a deputy in the National Assembly representing Bolomba and the only member of the opposition PUNA party in that body.

From the airport we traveled to the home of Jim and Maruja Conway. They live in embassy housing across the street from the train station. Dark falls at 6:30 this close to the equator and rises at 6:30 in the morning all year round. It was dark when we left the airport so I didn't see much of Kinshasa in the hour-long trip into town. Maruja had a light supper waiting for us when we got there. Inside the Conway's apartment is like being in the States. When you open the door, though, you're hit with the combination of odors—wood smoke, diesel, exotic cooking—that is the same throughout the developing world. I'll be staying with the Conways while I'm in Kinshasa. What a blessing.

On Friday we started with meetings in the USAID office, which is in the same complex as the Conway's apartment. There is great interest in our work. We then went with Jim and Simon Matula of the Food for Peace program and Dennis Basisulua, the president of Habitat for Humanity in Kinshasa, to Habitat's Mont Ngafula project where they have built 120 homes on a hillside. Dennis told us that Habitat now only sends money for administration and nothing for house building.

We left the Conways at 10:30 the next morning for the airport. Pierre was late so we finally left the compound at 11:15. An expediter from the embassy met us at the airport, took our passports and tickets in order to get our boarding passes. After a brief but rather intense encounter with airport police he got us inside the terminal where we left him to expedite. Expediters are the guardian angels of African travel. With that done we went through a cursory security check and into the VIP waiting room where we learned that the plane had been delayed. I met a Spanish-speaking Italian engineer who has lived in Africa his entire life and talked ceaselessly about everything that is wrong with the country and how much better things were under Mobutu. You wonder why he stays.

We finally left Kinshasa on Bravo Air Congo and 34 years almost to the day after Millard and Linda arrived here I set foot in Mbandaka. After waiting for yet another expediter we were driven to the provincial offices for a courtesy meeting with the Vice Governor, Jean Claude Baende Etafo Elika. I felt good about this man and believe that he will be helpful to us. He is quite young, mid-30s perhaps, though ages are deceiving here. He's a former Catholic priest and was educated in Belgium, which is where the governor is now. He comes from a small village east of Bolomba and could well be a major player in the Congolese politics in the future.

From there we were taken to Bokotola, a different site from one Millard worked at but given the same name. It was the second site in Mbandaka and work started there a few years after Millard and Linda left. Then we went to Losanganya where Millard and Linda built the first houses. I was able to call Millard on my cell phone and a crowd of neighbors shouted, "Millard—hello Millard." It was an emotional moment as this circle of his life was closed.

The DRC has been at war with itself for much of the time since it declared independence in 1960. Mbandaka was a major trading site for produce from the interior going to the Congo River and had a large Belgian community. It was probably a lovely town of sturdy buildings and tree-lined boulevards, but today it has the look of a post-apocalyptic city of hollow buildings where porches and terraces have become an outdoor market. There is a large central market with permanent stalls and concrete pillars for sunshades, but it stands empty while the streets around it are crowded with rickety thatch covered huts selling only the necessities. It's as though the area is reverting to a primitive, pre-colonial way of being. The houses in the Belgian quarter, which were separated from the African quarter by the no-man's land known as Bokotola, are now a squatter settlement of windowless shells whose former glory can only be discerned through the architecture.

The government offered us the use of a guesthouse on the waterfront and, coincidently, next door to the house the Fullers occupied when they lived here. As it turned out there were only three beds and no lights or mosquito nets, so Jim and

I decamped to the UN compound, MONUC, where we had clean sheets, running water, and access to the cafeteria. By the time we got there, though, the cafeteria had closed and a promised dinner at the governor's mansion failed to materialize so we set out in search of something to eat. It turns out that Mbandaka, a city of 70,000, has only one restaurant and they were hosting a wedding so they couldn't seat us. They sent us to an *auberge* which had only a few bottles of beer and coke, so we sent a couple of intrepid types out in search of anything. They returned with a few loaves of bread, which is quite good here, and two cans of corned beef. The *auberge* kitchen sliced the bread, untinned the corned beef, and *voilà*—dinner!

Saturday, July 8 my birthday

We got up at 5:30 for a 6:30 departure. The cafeteria wasn't open yet so we left without breakfast. After our meager repast of the night before we were a little peckish. We somehow snuck in a breakfast at the vice governor's house as atonement on his part for leaving us out of dinner the night before. We'd decided yesterday that the World Food Program boat would be too small and too slow so through the good offices of the vice governor we were offered the use of the Vodacom fast boat. Vodacom is a local cell phone company and their billboards along with those of Celltel and a couple of others are as ubiquitous throughout the country as Pepsi and Coke ads used to be. Naturally there were a few wrinkles. It turned out that the captain hadn't been given the final okay by the Vodacom manager so we got him out of bed to approve the use of the boat. We could only take six passengers and the battery was shot and the engine needed oil. There were no shops open so we bought some oil from the UNHCR (United Nations High Commissioner for Refugees), got the gas and battery from the World Food Program boat, trimmed the size of our entourage to six and by 9:15 we were ready to set sail. During the course of all these maneuverings we managed to score some bread and bananas so at least we'd have a little bit of lunch.

We set off up the Congo River towards the Ikalemba in the Vodacom boat—a great little launch built like a large canoe with a high powered motor that moved us like we were in a speedboat. It had a metal awning and permanent seats. The trip was long, but the visuals were incredible. We were in the heart of the jungle and the trees came right to the shoreline. There were numerous small thatched-hut villages along the way, many on stilts over the water. Most of them seemed abandoned, but they told me that these are fishing camps and the natives have more permanent houses deeper in the jungle. There were dugout canoes called pirogues of all sizes from small one man skiffs to huge transports. One of the big ones was carrying an overstuffed living room suite. Most of the people we did see waved as we passed by with both hands in the air and the kids jumped with excitement. There were some who were offended by our wake and sent less friendly waves our way.

We stopped part of the way in to drop off some tools to be used in building a school for Pygmy children and later stopped to pay a courtesy call on a local chieftain. It was a long trip – we left Mbandaka at 9:15 and arrived in Bolomba at 3:30 in the afternoon. We were greeted there by a couple hundred folks and a military police attachment. One of our party, M. Adbokuma Ngale, is the provincial minister of agriculture and he was the reason for the military salute. The rest were there to greet the white men. They told us that Jim and I were the first of our tribe to visit Bolomba in over 20 years. In addition to Jim, M. Ngale, and me our party included the Hon. Pierre Maloka, Simon Mutula of the Food for Peace Program and Jean Pierre Alemboa, a Bolomban who lives in Mbandaka and works for Maloka. His name will come up again.

We left the river in a grand and long procession to what passes for the center of town. There we were subjected to much speechifying and Maloka was the star of the show. I spoke a little about the Fuller Center. We then walked en masse to the site by the river that is being donated by a local chief for the first houses. It looks like a nice parcel, well above the river and quite flat. We then went to the guest house for dinner. I'm not quite sure what it was – most African meats seem to be mostly gristle and bone. I can't figure out what the animals that produce such meat must look like. There was rice and three types of greens, one manioc leaves, two spinach, I think. It was a gracious gesture on the part of our hosts.

We were then taken by motorbike to the Catholic compound where we were to spend the night. No lights, no water, no bedding, no mosquito nets but a good roof and a bed. I was grateful to have my sleeping bag and flashlight. The compound, which includes a church, a school, a small seminary, and the guest house, was used as a base by the Bemba forces during the Civil War. Bolomba was on the front lines during the conflict and towards the end of the war Kabila's forces bombed the church, leaving little more than a foundation and a few pillars. The Bemba troops then stole the ferry and disappeared down the river

Our original plan was to spend two days in Bolomba, but Bravo Air changed their schedule and we had to leave a day early leaving only the morning to meet with the locals and start setting things up. The committee was set to arrive at eight so we met at nine. There was a tremendous storm during the night which accounts I'm sure for the tardiness. There were some 12 folks who will be the steering committee led by Pastor Moloko, the Baptist pastor. We talked for some time about what it will take to start a project. I'd hoped to have them divide into three committees—got two, family selection and construction. No one came forward to work on the land issues, but the minister of agriculture put his staff on that part which is fine as it will mostly be technical work—platting, topos, soil tests and the like.

A dynamic leader didn't emerge, so we have contracted with Jean Pierre Alemboa to keep things moving. By now it was mid-morning and we were anxious to get on the river so that we could make it back to Mbandaka before dark. The priest and seminarians had prepared breakfast for us so we ate and were motorbiked back to the beach. We were finally all aboard except for Jean Pierre, who was missing in action. So we cruised up the river to try to find him, unsuccessfully as it turned out. We went back to the beach and he finally showed up. He'd been collecting a supply of smoked monkeys for Maloka to bring to Kinshasa. This was a true *Out of Africa* experience. He put the bag in the front of the boat, right in front of me. Before long the bag sagged open leaving me to stare directly at the poor little things, which were propped up on the cross-like devices they'd been smoked on. Eerie. I was finally able to get the bag closed so I didn't have to watch them anymore. There was some karmic justice at work though— when we got back to Kinshasa we found that someone had stolen the monkeys from the overhead bin on the plane.

We left Bolomba at about 12:15 and sped down the river. We stopped briefly to visit a local chief but he was away. We stopped again to deliver some forgotten materials along with Jean Pierre to the Pygmy landing. We actually saw some Pygmies this time—they were a motley crew. Turns out they are the oppressed people here in this oppressed place—go figure. We got back to Mbandaka at about 5:30 with plenty of light. The vice governor wanted us to come to dinner so we cleaned up—got the folks at MONUC to give us each a tub of hot water for a bath, delivered in buckets. Then off to the vice governor's house for a lovely dinner. The Congo does have a richer cuisine then Nigeria.

We learned that the Bravo Air flight to Kinshasa was now delayed from 11:30 in the morning to 4:30 in the afternoon so we had some time to do some visiting.

We met the UN civil affairs officer, a Togolese, and the UN head of office, a Senegalese. Conway met with some of his World Food Project folks and I mostly tagged along. We got to the airport at 3:30 to learn that the plane was further delayed. It finally arrived and was ready to board at 5:30. It was a typical Third World boarding process—lots of pushing and general panic. Turns out that Bravo Air typically overbooks so panic is a required part of the process. We assumed ourselves into the VIP line and then on to the front of the plane where the flight attendant motioned us into first class seats. This is a flight of less than an hour and they had food service—chicken and rice upfront, two sandwiches in the rear. Interesting.

Back in Kinshasa—had a free morning and went in the afternoon with the Habitat folks to visit their Mpasa site out past the airport. Pretty bleak. The houses there are smaller—about 400 square feet—three rooms, two bedrooms and one living, cooking outside, and a latrine out back. Apparently the Habitat folks in South Africa got wind of my visit so I was asked to low profile it—apparently they're still afraid that we might steal their sheep. We stopped at a local eatery on the way out of the project site. I had *mbisi maboke*, which is fish steamed in large leaves (very good) and *chikwangue*, which is cassava bread (awful).

The next day we left the house at 9:30 to go to the docks and get the embassy boat to Brazzaville. There were three of us on the boat – Jim, a CIA operative, and me. We got across with no problems – left our papers with yet another expediter who must've had a hard time of it as we didn't see our passports again until the afternoon. We went straight to the American embassy, which is temporarily housed in a bank building. Apparently the embassy was closed here for a number of years. A new building is going up.

We met with ambassador Weisberg and two representatives from the Christian Missionary Alliance, David Bill and Charles Bemba, and an embassy rep named Landry. We talked in general terms. The ambassador would like to see us build for some teachers and also has some government land we may be able to get on a 99-year lease. Neither option quite fits our model.

I like the ambassador. He's full of energy and wants to do something. He's charged with rebuilding a presence here but only has a staff of six. They have something like 13 cars but only two drivers. He's clearly a broad stroke guy, though—details are for others, such as myself, to attend to. We left the embassy and visited two schools that could be candidates for teacher housing, one was a high school with 1,400 students, the second the primary school with 3,900 students.

I can't see where either facility, both in truly deplorable conditions, could physically accommodate even a third of the students there.

We then went to the embassy parcel which looks like a prime piece of real estate. It sits on the bluff overlooking the river next-door to the French ambassador's house. If we can sort through the lease issues, we may be able to put 20 to 25 houses there. We then went to our lodging, which used to be the ambassador's residence— not at all shabby. We went to lunch at a Lebanese place. I had a wrap—very good, then shopping for a few staples—very expensive. There's a large Lebanese population in Brazzaville and they apparently control a good deal of the business.

That afternoon we went to the Villa Washington, which is the embassy's youth outreach facility housed at the former American Club, to attend a meeting of the English Club. The French ambassador was the guest speaker and gave a forthright presentation on French-African relations. They asked me to speak so I spoke about self-reliance and personal responsibility. We then went to the French Cultural Center for a backstage visit to a concert. The crowd outside the gate was not happy to see us waved in and I actually caught someone reaching into my hip pocket. I was able to dissuade their larcenous intent. We listened to a group called Seth Shark, an Icelandic group with a black American-Icelandic lead singer, a South African conga player and a Congolese drummer. Interesting. We had a late dinner at a place called Mami Wata, which sits right on the Corniche overlooking the river. Brazzaville actually has a *corniche*, an elegant stretch of road along the river.

We had a gentle start today. We went to visit the new embassy site, which was a little galling. There are three perfectly good block buildings there that apparently are just for the construction phase and will be torn down once the embassy itself is built. Such a waste. We spent the afternoon visiting two sites where the International Partnership for Human Development has renovated schools, one at Kambi and the other at Makana. Both are on the Pool road toward Kinkala. We're going back to Makana on Monday to meet with the people there. Something could develop from this visit.

Another quiet day. Jim went back to Kinshasa and I went into town to do some shopping. Prices are exorbitant here due, I'm told, to the difficulties of getting things imported. Most of the goods come through Pointe Noir. The road is virtually impassable, so it all comes by rail on a failing system. I spent the afternoon at the house and then went to the French ambassador's for the Bastille Day celebration. A staid event—lots of diplomats and government types. A local choir sang a powerful rendition of the *Marseillaise*. Brazzaville was the capital of Free France for a time during World War II. I could picture de Gaulle coming down the steps of the Ambassador's house. Food was pretty much cheese and pâté with some delicious mini desserts. Sunday was Election Day and the city was closed to motor traffic. I was advised to stay home. I did go over to the Bills for lunch—they live just down the street. It was a long, long day.

The next morning I met with representatives from the embassy and the Christian Missionary Association to talk about the project and what would be required to set up a local organization. We then drove to Makana, which is outside of Brazzaville in the Pool province. The road out of Brazzaville is in terrible repair, but once outside the city it improves greatly. Turns out that the Chinese have built a new highway there in exchange, I'm told, for vast timber rights. This is apparently something that they're doing throughout Africa—offering major public works in exchange for long-term access to resources.

Makana spreads out along the highway and doesn't have much of a village feel. We visited some of the potential home sites. The Pool was a hotbed during the civil war and a number of the houses were bombed out. The rebels, called Ninjas, are apparently still somewhat active, but we fortunately didn't encounter any. We ended by meeting with the village leaders. They are very interested in doing something and waiting for word on how to proceed. We ended the meeting with a palm wine toast. Not bad.

I had dinner with Allie Lloyd and Phil Barth. They're here working on the new embassy. She's with the contractor; he's with the budget office. They're both good Christian folks and I had hopes that one of them might take the lead on the project, but it was not meant to be. Allie will help with the house design through an NGO she works with—Engineering Ministries out of Colorado Springs, my home town, of all places. Both pretty much went into a fugue state when I suggested they get more involved.

Another day, another slow start. I didn't hear from anyone at the Embassy so I got a cab to head over that way. The driver took me to the old embassy and then couldn't find the new one. It was kind of frightening actually because the old embassy is on the edge of town and we were driving down back streets to get there. For a minute I thought maybe my time had come. I was able to muster enough French to get us back in the right direction, but the cabby wasn't very happy with the extra mileage. I figured it was pretty much his fault.

I met with the ambassador and a Catholic bishop from Kinshasa, and a representative from the Papal Nuncio's office. Both were very gracious and the bishop pledged his support. The Nuncio, Monsignor Kuruake, is the bishop over Pool so Makana is in his See. He invited me to meet with their construction people. Ina, a wonderful woman who was my embassy escort, then treated me to lunch—good chicken, awful couscous—and brought me home. I met in the afternoon with more people to talk about setting up a program but no one has come forward yet to lead the effort. At 4:00 a Vatican car took me to their embassy where I met with Father Luciano Acquisto. He and the Monsignor have shown the most interest in our work, yet neither is in a position to lead. Fr. Luciano will be a great resource on the construction side. Then dinner at seven at the ambassador's new house—very good pizza. The house is quite grand, fitting for the American presence here.

Yet another quiet morning. I got invited to David Bill's for lunch but I'd already eaten so went just to say goodbye. His U.S. delegation had arrived and I got to meet John Stumbo, the president of the CMA from Colorado Springs. Will hook up again when we get home. Maybe we can fire them up. Ina then took me to the embassy for a goodbye meeting with the ambassador. I think he's disappointed that we aren't starting a project next week but until we find some leadership we really can't pull things together. I left at 3:00 for the boat – pure chaos at both ends. Thank goodness for Embassy expediters. I am back at Conway's – an oasis. Maloka came by for a visit and he's taking me to the National Assembly tomorrow.

Pierre picked me up at nine. We stopped by an art dealer near his home, but the prices seemed high to me based on what Conway has collected. We then went to the Parliament building where the Senate and National Assembly meet. I'm told that the building, which is huge, was Mobutu Sese Seko's party headquarters during his three-decade dictatorship.   Maloka represents Bolomba in the Assembly. The session ended last night. It's the first truly elected assembly in the country's history. I met with some of Maloka's fellow Equator District delegates and members FONAPO—not sure what that stands for. I got back in time for an 11 o'clock debrief with USAID. From there to the Air France office nearby to drop off luggage and get the pre-board taken care of.

Had a lovely dinner with the Conways then off to the airport. Traffic was a disaster. Got there in time to go straight to passport control. Security took a half hour but I made my flight and I'm heading home.

Thursday, January 24, 2008

Once again I find myself in the Colorado Springs airport preparing for another jaunt. This will be like none before it—four countries in three weeks requiring 13 different flights on five separate carriers. If I walk through this terminal on February 12 with myself and my stuff intact it will only be through divine intervention!

I started making plans for this trip a little late so I probably own the difficulties that ensued. And they have been manifold. They started with the difficulties my travel agent at Siddhi had in making the on-the-ground arrangements in Africa. The original plan was to go from the DRC to Nigeria, on to Ghana and then home. Simple enough. But getting from Kinshasa to Abuja means taking an Air Ivoire flight to Abidjan then a Cameroon Airlines flight to Lagos and a Virgin Nigeria flight to Abuja. Getting from Abuja to Accra is a little simpler—United Airlines to Lagos and then United again to Accra

So we had this all worked out when the time came to get visas and I realized I had scheduled a trip to El Salvador that would tie my passport up for a vital week. So I got with the folks at the visa agency, who said they could get all of the visas except the one for the Republic of Congo, which would take four days. Not a problem says I—I could get that in Kinshasa. About halfway through the process I got a call advising me that the DRC embassy had inexplicably closed and wouldn't reopen until after I was scheduled to leave. So we regrouped and they rushed through the ROC visa in a day, after all, and I made arrangements to fly into Brazzaville instead of Kinshasa. This meant changing my departure from the 24th to the 25th, which was fine as I'd barely gotten everything done that needed doing as it was. It also meant changes on the ground in the Congo, about which my old friend Jim Conway was none too happy.

So now the plan is that I arrive Friday evening in Brazzaville, spend the weekend doing Makana business, and on Monday rush around getting my DRC visa worked out and confirming the Air Ivoire Cameroon A/L flights. If I were able to get the DRC visa on Monday (the US embassy says no problem) then on Tuesday I'll fly to Mbandaka so we can head up river to Bolomba. And this is just the first leg! Then it's on to Abuja and Accra. Goodness.

In the meantime I've asked for $3,500 to cover the ground expenses and to open a bank account in Kinshasa. I get the check and take it to the bank and they want to put a five-day hold on it. After what appeared to be intensive consultation they agreed to release the funds. One more dragon slain, one more anxiety quieted.

When I get to the Colorado Springs airport it turns out that in their zeal my travel agent has booked me on at least three flights out. It takes two gate agents to sort it all out. At this point I'm confirmed on both the transatlantic flights, coming and going but the only assigned seat I've got is the one for the first leg of the trip. In Atlanta it took two more gate agents to get me a boarding pass to Paris – they issued the Brazzaville pass with a coupon requirement so I have to sort that out in Paris. This will be a step-by-step trip.

I made it to Paris on January 25 uneventfully. I had a great deal of trouble finding Concourse C—turns out it involves a bus trip. De Gaulle has moved to the bottom of my favorability list for international airports. We got in at 6 o'clock in the morning—nothing opens before 8. I found a gate agent who was able to fix my boarding pass and left for Brazzaville without difficulty but 40 minutes late.

I got to Brazzaville at 7 PM and had an escort waiting to walk me through passport control and get the luggage. Joe O'Brien and crew brought me to the Hotel du Boulevard and here I sit, 9:45 PM local time, waiting for a bite to eat. I called Jim Conway and he's glad I've made it this far. Called home—Sheilla had been waiting to hear. Now a bite to eat, a good night's sleep and onward.

The next day was a long and empty one. I had breakfast in the hotel – very European, cold cuts and hard-boiled eggs, passable coffee and, as always here, great bread. Joe picked me up around 10 o'clock and we went to his office where we met Dr. Gemba. I got my first look at the house plans and materials take-offs. We're looking at $12,000 to $13,000 for a 450-square-foot house. Shocking. This is going to take some serious discussion. We're supposed to meet again tomorrow with more of the team to discuss this and then we're going out to Makana.

Joe took me to the Brazza monument—stunning, over-the-top really. Brazza's family is buried there but there are rumors President Sassou intends to replace them when he goes. The place is built like the Parthenon and is all marble, imported from Italy they say. It's really spectacular and totally out of place in a land of such poverty. We had lunch at Nouras, a Lebanese place I've been to before. Then back to the hotel where I spent the afternoon reading and napping. Joe picked me up for dinner at seven. We went to a place near the embassy.

The economy here seems to be driven in part by the collapsed transportation system. The highway and railroad between Brazzaville and Pointe Noir on the coast are in serious disrepair, which drives up the cost of everything as most everything but manioc is imported.

As it turned out this was a very good day. I was concerned that the construction cost issue might derail the project, but after speaking this morning with Allie and Charles we started to get our arms around the issue. We were facing two issues—the size of the house and the materials. Their plans called for a very nice three-bedroom home built of cement block. We started by taking apart the house plans. The thinking had been that the families need three bedrooms for cultural reasons, the boys in one, the girls in another, and mom and dad in the third. This does make sense, but when you're building with a family that lives in a one room shack and can afford maybe a $10 monthly payment, there are practical issues that need to come into play. I think that part of the problem is like we had with some in El Salvador—the charitable impulse to give coupled with the liberal approach of using other people's money. We talked it through and I explained how it would limit by at least half our capacity and that raising the U.S. dollars for a $13,000 house would be difficult. So we redesigned and came up with a much simpler plan shaving 20 to 30% off the cost. Still too high but heading in the right direction.

We left about noon for Makana – Joe, Dr. Ngama, Charles, Allie, Jim Conroy from our team and the new Deputy Chief of Mission Cynthia along with Kelly and Russell from the embassy. There were 35 to 40 people waiting for us and we had a great meeting. Dr. Ngama presided. I don't know what he told them, but the unanimous decision of the group was to build two-bedroom homes using stabilized mud bricks rather than cement block. Suddenly our house cost issues were resolved. It looks like there are 30 to 35 houses in Makana, most in bad shape. I believe that just about every household was represented. The opportunity we have here is to eliminate poverty housing in one discrete area and create a model that can be used in other parts of the country. The basic requirements are decent homes, hygienic latrines, water wells and rainwater recovery. If we can do that for an entire community, we will be off to a huge start.

We toured the village and then started back to Brazzaville. We stopped at a brick making operation near Makana. I learned that we can buy clay bricks for 50 francs versus 350 francs each for cement. We stopped at Les Rapides just outside of Brazzaville on the way back. This is where the Congo River ceases to be navigable. We watched the kids ride the rapids in inner tubes. We had dinner at Mama Wati's, which apparently is creole for mermaid, down on the riverfront. Not bad, buffet style, but still a little pricey.

Picking up the pieces today. I had to rearrange the Nigeria leg because we get back from Mbandaka after I'm scheduled to leave for Lagos. I got a new ticket—direct from Kinshasa to Lagos—which will save the grief of Air Ivoire to Abidjan and Cameron Airlines to Lagos. It cuts my Nigeria stay short and I'll miss church with Sam Odia on Sunday. I'll speak at the International Church in Kinshasa instead. We were able to confirm a UNHCR (United Nations High Commissioner for Refugees) flight to Mbandaka.

I had lunch with the ambassador. He's hanging it up after just two years—a shame really for him as he's got to have a certain sense of leaving a job only partly done, and for the Republic of the Congo. Maybe he couldn't do any more than he did but I'm surprised that he's leaving.

A little rest in the afternoon—my Mama Wati meal didn't sit too well. Back to the embassy in the afternoon to watch the video on the U.S. Navy Seabees' school rehab project and then to dinner at *Orchidée*—very nice, very French and not too pricey. Home late and then repacking for the Bolomba trip. Conway is taking my big bag to Kinshasa.

Up early to the airport for the UNHCR plane. We fly to Kinshasa where we will pick up Pierre Maloka then on to Mbandaka. So far so good. Pierre was ready and waiting and we got back on our way with no difficulties. Strange: no passport control on the DRC side—I hope that doesn't screw up my departure. Good flight to Mbandaka—slow, we were on a Czech turboprop—but a smooth trip. Apparently every airport in the Congo thinks of itself as international so I had to go through the formalities which involved once again getting my passport to an expediter and waiting. In this case I had to find the visa page for them and point out that it actually said Democratic Republic of the Congo. Life is strange here. We went straight from the airport to the vice governor's office. He continues to be interested in this project and wants to go with us to Bolomba, which is good, because we will arrive there in style and it doesn't hurt to have a big man on your side. The downside is that we won't leave until Thursday, so we have to kill a day in Mbandaka and we lose a day and Bolomba. When we met he greeted me by shaking hands and touching the side of my forehead to his, right then left then right again—a gracious greeting.

We finally got to our lodging at the UN base, MONUC, at about 2 o'clock in the afternoon and ate fish cooked in manioc leaves. Not bad accommodations, though, for $40 a night. Pierre, Jean Pierre and I spent the time going over the status of the project. That status is that 25 families have been selected and have given 35,000 francs down (about $50), we have seven hectares (about 17 acres) donated which will accommodate 250 houses. We'll start with 25 and then another 25.

Dinner tonight at the vice governor's house. An interesting tidbit on our trip to his office—the president of the Chamber of Commerce is an ever-present figure in our dealings here in Mbandaka. I always get the feeling he's looking for an angle. Anyway he was aghast that I would consider visiting the vice governor without a jacket and tie, so much so that he took off his own tie and made me wear it. So I attended the meeting looking like some goof from a bad 40s movie. Life in Africa—never without surprises.

Today is a dead day in Mbandaka. We're going to visit a cocoa plantation and stop by the equator monument. I want to go back to Losanganya for some more photos. Beyond that I'm not sure what the day will bring. We had dinner last night at the vice governor's—he's moved into an official residence, a restored colonial villa. A villa here is a single-family, detached house with enough room for a yard enclosed by a wall. There are definite signs of improvement here. The government house is much cleaner and is being fixed up. Some of the streets are being repaired—small things, but that's a start. An exception is MONUC, which seems to be in decline. It could be due to a reduced UN presence, but things here don't seem as sharp and disciplined as they were.

Dinner was interesting. The same food as always—manioc leaves cooked with dried fish, and unidentifiable joints of unidentifiable meats, beef skewers, rice and fish cooked in giant leaves. And pounded manioc—not my cup of tea. The formalities are serious, though. We were ushered to an outdoor pavilion by Secret Service types—plainclothes police I imagine. After a while we were taken into the living room where we watched Nigeria beat Benin in the African soccer games. There was a very pretty young lady there who looked to be about 14. Nothing was said but it was hard for me not to worry about her. Matters of the heart are a bit murky on this side of the pond.

Dinner was eaten in silence until I reached a breaking point and had some insightful questions, like why the vice governor has three cell phones (one for each of the local networks) or how long he's been in the new home (two months). Despite the strange dynamics, to my lighthearted American eye, a grand time was had by all. I began to fade and claimed tiredness due to my advanced age and the evening ended.

Maloka joined me for breakfast and we met with Madame Terrunane Anciene, whom I met last July in Kinshasa, where she was heading up Habitat for Humanity. She was let go and has moved to Mbandaka to start an NGO to deal with a wide range of issues. It appears to be unfunded and seems to lack focus. Maloka is trying to help her identify a single cause, possibly improving the toilet situation throughout Mbandaka. Habitat shut down here in the DRC at the end of 2007—I wish they'd have let us know so we could have picked up the pieces.

It's 4:30 now and I'm back at MONUC. Our field trip is over. We left here about 9:30 in the morning and went to Maloka's inn, the Rock of Ages, to wait for the vehicle that the vice governor had promised. By 10:30, and after lots of calls, Pierre took off with Jean Pierre and the irritating little guy from the Chamber leaving me with a pair of very nice pastors who wanted to visit. I believe the African-American and Congolese churches should come together to preach the gospel. I said that the American church is a little preoccupied these days with social issues but the African church seems to be prospering. By now it was 11:30 and the pastors and I were drifting into uncomfortable silences, so I retreated back to MONUC. A little after noon Pierre, the Chamber of Commerce guy, and I headed out of Dodge to visit a cocoa plantation. I told Pierre that as there was no cocoa in Bolomba my interest was in coffee. We really didn't have to make the trip, but apparently most of official Mbandaka was committed to getting me to the cocoa trees so the die was cast. We drove south out of Mbandaka past the Disciples of Christ complex, where Maloka went to school, then turned east and drove into the jungle for two hours. I'd wanted to stop at the equator site and get a picture but someone has stolen the sign so I missed that opportunity

We passed through a Pygmy funeral procession and village after village of daub and wattle and mud brick houses. These houses don't have chimneys and smoke from the cooking fires goes out through the eaves. I worry for the lungs of the children living in there. Every now and again we paused so they could point out a coconut tree or abandoned palm oil plantation. Our driver acted like the devil was on his tail and drove at great speed with horn honking past bicyclists and pedestrians who scurried out of the way. He did hit a goat, and maybe a kid goat, which angered and saddened me. All told it was a grim adventure except for the road itself, which was remarkably good. There were even repair crews out in a couple of places driving brand new trucks with the EU flag on the side. After two hours or so the road forked with one branch heading for Kinshasa, the other for

DAVID SNELL

Bolomba and points east. Apparently the road deteriorates badly after that so getting to either place is a major undertaking. The fork is at a place called Karamba! We never did get to see a cocoa plantation. We did walk into one that has gone wild and saw some sad looking seedlings. Good thing I wasn't too interested.

Now we're making plans for the Bolomba trip. I'm expected to pay for the gasoline at a cost of about $600 plus, which strikes me as odd. That translates to 100 gallons at local prices. Bolomba is at most 130 miles away, 260 round-trip, which means we'll make less than 3 miles per gallon. In the meantime I have to rely on Maloka to confirm my return flight with UNHCR. At this point we don't know what time it will be leaving from here on Saturday. On a positive note I was able to connect with Sam Odia in Nigeria, so that leg is worked out. Step by slogging step.

A number of the Bolomba folks are here in town today and tracked Maloka down. We arranged that he would call by six to let me know if I should eat at MONUC or if we had an invite. About 6:15 Jean Pierre stopped by to take me over to Maloka's, which became the meeting place with the Bolomba group. The chief was there along with the head of the schools and the deputy sheriff. They are interested in education, health, transportation routes and economic development I keep asserting that we're not here to do those things but rather to be a catalyst for others. We visited until eight, came back to MONUC to eat and found that the cafeteria was closed. So Pierre and I walked into town and had fish and fried plantains at an open-air restaurant in the Joseph Kabila Park. There doesn't seem to be any power in this town and it was a moonless night so we ate by flashlight. There are very few private cars here—most of the traffic is on foot or bicycle.

A note about the UN presence here: I'm staying in the MONUC (United Nations Mobilization Center in the DRC, or something along those lines) compound, which is their northern headquarters. They seem to have a number of interests based on the names over the reserved parking stalls—a radio station, human rights, health, and military. They have a huge investment in rolling stock—they're probably the ones who put Toyota over the top in world-wide sales. Maloka isn't real sure what they're doing here and would like to see them go. There are lots of troops, mostly African. I've seen Ghanaians and Nigerians and others. I visited with some Uruguayans. Apparently the Germans have gone home—they couldn't deal with the relaxed approach to timeliness here. The MPs all seem to be Bangladeshis. It's not a bad place to stay—24-hour electricity, running water (cold), and intense security. As one with limited affection for the United Nations I mostly see waste.

92

Thursday, January 31, 2008, today we go to Bolomba, which is pretty much the reason for this whole trip. We only get a day on the ground there because the vice governor is coming and we're going on his boat. It turns out that the boat actually belongs to President Kabila. It's a speedboat and should make for a fast trip. And it did—we arrived in Bolomba in record time.

It's evening now and we're staying in the government guest house, which the vice governor thought would be safer than the seminary. An interesting day. We figured we'd leave Mbandaka by 10 o'clock. By 10:30 we were sitting under the pavilion at the vice governor's residence. By 11:30 we moved to the quay at the governor's mansion. We were underway at 12:40. The governor's is a speed boat with an under-deck cabin and a 200 hp V6 engine. It cut two hours off the trip. We got here just after 3:00 in the afternoon. Good thing too as most of the official party were stuck in the cabin. I lucked out and got assigned a seat above deck so I put on my iPod and sped down the Ikalemba with John Denver, Andrea Bocelli, and Enya keeping me company. Aside from the fact that we were on a floating gasoline bomb with five gallon jugs stacked everywhere it was a glorious trip. The jungle is lovely, dark and deep and you just can't stop looking at it. You're seldom out of sight of humanity. There are villages all along the river and pirogues everywhere. All these people coming and going – you have to wonder what they're all up to. With some it's clear—big loads of wood aboard or fish traps. Most are an enigma. Folks along the shore would wave Congo style with both arms in the air. Kids would race out on smaller pirogues to ride our wake. Every now and then someone would wave a fist at us as though our passing were an offense. I'm sure they'd say the same if they were suddenly dropped on any American freeway.

We arrived in Bolomba at about 3 o'clock. The vice governor had sent a pirogue ahead loaded with gasoline for the return trip and his personal food—he doesn't eat with the locals. I tried to sit next to the V-G whenever we ate because he had a big tub of peanut butter with him and that, with the delicious bread, was a way for me to fill my stomach while enjoying smaller bites of the delicacies I was offered. On this trip I was served crocodile as a special treat.

There was a large delegation including a fife and drum band and honor guard to meet us along with most of the population of Bolomba. From the quay we walked and walked to the government center, where the elite among us were installed in overstuffed chairs on the porch. I'm not sure what the purpose of this phase of the operation was. I do know that I was parched and hot and anxiously awaiting the refreshment that never came. After an hour of this we were loaded onto the back of a pickup truck for a 40-minute trip out to the new airport site. Apparently the vice governor was less than pleased with the progress he was hoping for so it wasn't a happy trip.

We got back to the guest house at six and resumed our places of honor on the porch. By this time my need for something—anything—was reaching critical mass. So I broke into the vice governor's travel goodies and had a little picnic. At dinner that night the vice governor, who had brought his own tableware and food, kept me close. I ate light but well. We were staying in the government guest house which had power and water. My room had two pieces of furniture—an unmade bed (which I would have made up but there was nothing to make it up with)—and an outboard motor. And the lights didn't work. I slept well though. It was hotter than blazes when we first retired but halfway through the night it cooled off. I was grateful to have my sleeping bag. I was awakened around five by an unmelodious Muslim calling me to prayer. I finally got up at six, cleaned up some with a bucket of water I was given, and here I sit making notes and trying to avoid the stares of the guards who want cigarettes.

We had breakfast with the vice governor, Maloka, the sheriff (who I believe is the local administrator) and others. We talked about coffee and initiatives. I pointed out to the vice governor, as we were stirring our coffee from a tin of instant from Belgium, that we could reach out the window and harvest coffee beans from an abandoned bush. I asked the vice governor if there was any particular message he wanted me to share. His answer – the gravy train has stopped. As a counterpoint when I thanked the breakfast ladies they told me that if I were truly grateful I could give them some money. Small steps.

After my encounter with the cooks they sent for me to come to the town center where a festival was underway. There was a huge crowd—several hundred—and the vice governor was telling them how the cow ate the cabbage. He berated the local leadership for misappropriating the money that had been sent for roadwork and the police for harassing people and over-fining. This last bit had me a little concerned as the only thing between us and an angry mob was the police. This was all being done in Lingala so the little I got of it came through Maloka. The basic message was that accountability is back and the people need to take part in getting things done. No more free lunch. Interesting in a place where people expect so little from the government in the first place and get less. But he is clearly taken with the notions of self-help and personal responsibility.

From there we headed to the building site where an awning had been set up for the first stone (ground breaking) and ribbon cutting. The whole event was formal and joyless—no singing or dancing. Then the national anthem was played by the fife and drum corps with military honors. The sheriff welcomed everyone, and the V-G, Maloka and Alemboa all spoke. I shared a few words—there was apparently some jealousy about the family selection so in my remarks I told them that our goal is for every child in Bolomba to have a decent place to live. This did get some applause. I told them that we are just beginning, step-by-step—*moko, moko, moko*. We then went to lay the first stone and cut the ribbon. The vice governor dedicated the site and the street names. The first stone was laid at the corner of Snell Ave. and Maloka St.

We had a big parade back to town and Maloka, Alemboa, and I broke off with the Fuller Center board. We went to their office for a short meeting. Someone graciously arrived with cut pineapple which I devoured—the most refreshing event of the entire trip. We then broke up and headed to the quay. We left at 1:40 and arrived back at the governor's mansion at about six. The cabinet was there to receive the vice governor and we all went to his house for sodas and beers. Maloka, Alemboa, and I were invited to stay for dinner. Maloka feels that it was a perfect trip. He says that the vice governor is very taken with our model and wants to expand it into other aspects of community life. His messages in Bolomba were consistent in pushing self-help and individual initiative. He challenged the people there to come up with a draft proposal on coffee production by the end of the month for me to take to "my people". He also challenged them to have the runway cleared by March.

It was a good trip all in all—hot, dirty and tiring, but a success. I had a moment of anxiety at MONUC—the Ukrainian Civil Air Force was there and told me that our UNHCR plane was out of commission. That affected my sleep. It turned out that it was the other UNHCR plane that was out of service so we got in the air heading for Brazzaville and then on to Kinshasa. Providence stepped in yet once again. I'm not sure what I could've done about Nigeria if we were stuck in Mbandaka until the next week. All is well.

The trip turned into a long one – we went from Mbandaka to Brazzaville and got hung up there for an hour waiting for clearance. We got to Kinshasa okay and hitched a ride on a UN car into town. The traffic was bad. I went to an embassy party with the Conways and didn't get home until midnight.

I slept like the innocent last night. We're going to the International Church today. I'll have a chance to speak, then a quiet afternoon. It will be nice to just be at peace for a few hours. We left early for church—Jim's watch was running 20 minutes fast. We hung around while the French service ended. The English service started at 11:30. It's the International Protestant Church in Kinshasa—nondenominational and a little charismatic for my tastes. I spoke briefly about the Bolomba project. It's a small church, mostly missionary kids who have never left the Congo. I'm not sure much will come of the visit. We then went to the café Mozart for quiche but there wasn't any so I ordered a ham and cheese sandwich which came to me as tuna. Great bread. The café is run by nuns who take girls off the street and train them in service (poorly) and baking bread (very well). We then went to the Grand Hotel in search of a DRC flag. Maruja knows some people there. I did get a flag—not exactly what I was looking for but a start. We were there for some time as Maruja tried to locate some people she was supposed to meet. From there we went to Maloka's where we found him in fine form—no wheels, no phone, but rested from the trip and ready to go. He has a compound near the presidential mansion and there were people coming and going the whole time we were there. We gave Jim a trip update and made some plans. Pierre is very pleased with what we did in Bolomba.

Our last stop was a convent of the Franciscan sisters of Mary where, remarkably, everyone seemed to speak Spanish so I was able to actually visit. They have a project some 100 km outside of Kinshasa where they'd like to build some houses. I don't know what will come of it but I'll send them some information.

So now I'm in the airport in Kinshasa awaiting a flight to Lagos. This leg of the trip is coming to an end. It's been just over a week since I arrived in Brazzaville but it seems like a lifetime. A week from today I begin my journey home—two stops along the way: Abuja and Accra. I have been blessed. Most of the major travel challenges are now behind me. On to Nigeria.

October, 2008

We just got a great report from Jean Pierre Alemboa, who heads up the project in Bolomba, Democratic Republic of Congo, so I'm copying it below.

Rapport d'activites Sur Le Déroulement des Travaux de Construction des Maisons Fuller Center for Housing Bolomba: Depuis l'ouverture de site de Fuller Center For Housing Bolomba par la pose de la 1ère pierre jusqu'à présent on reconnaît les activités suivantes:

Did you get that? The DRC was once the Belgian Congo, and in addition to learning how to make a great loaf of bread, the *Congolaise* picked up French as their common language (this in addition to over 100 local languages spoken throughout the country). This works well for them, but has me challenged. I'm trying to pick up a word or two, but languages are best learned in one's youth. Fortunately we have friends who are fluent in French and translated Jean Pierre's report—

Report of the Construction Work Activities of The Fuller Center for Housing in Bolomba, Democratic Republic of the Congo (DRC)

Since the laying of the first stone at the dedication of the Fuller Center for Housing in Bolomba, the following activities have taken place:

CLEARING OF THE FOREST

The team assigned to clearing and surveying the site has already begun work. They delimited the site of The Fuller Center project using avenues as borders; among these are avenues honoring David Snell and the Honorable Pierre Maloka, which were dedicated by the vice governor of the province. The team divided the site of phase one--a total of 700 square meters which we obtained from the village of Bosanjo—into 23 parcels of 30 square meters each.

The clearing of the land is hard work in Bolomba because of the sheer immensity of the forest and the large trees which must be cut down before the start of any other work. All of this has been finished.

SITE PLAN

Each parcel of land measures 30 square meters and will have a two, three or four-room house with an exterior toilet. All selected beneficiaries are already working on their own plots. The beneficiaries are preparing their land by clearing bush, cutting down trees, removing stumps and roots. They collect and burn this waste to prepare the land for the house foundations. Again, this is a very hard task because the large trees must be cut down with axes, not just machetes.

This work of clearing the forest and burning waste can only be done during the dry season. To further complicate matters at the equator there are no real seasons and it can rain at any moment. The beneficiaries put their heart and soul into their work on dry days, before sudden rains arrive.

THE BRICK MAKING SHEDS

The beneficiaries who have finished clearing their land are already building sheds for brick-making. These sheds are constructed with trees, vines and thatch that are cut or purchased, and this takes several weeks.

One should note that work in the DRC is different from Congo Brazzaville (Republic of Congo) because in Brazzaville, there is mostly desert-like land and small trees which can be cut and burned in one day, whereas in the DRC, there are large trees and dense forests which must be cleared with axes. Another difference is that the Makana project (of The Fuller Center project in the Republic of Congo/Brazzaville) is close to the capital city where one can find everything needed for construction. Getting supplies poses no problems in Makana, but in Bolomba, we must travel to Kinshasa for supplies and we lack adequate transportation. In spite of this, the site has been prepared and is ready for construction.

THE BRICKS

The bricks are already being made with the aid of presses which we obtained from The Honorable Pierre Maloka Makonzi. Two teams have been formed to make bricks. Certain sheds already contain bricks that are ready to fire and several kilns have already been constructed and are ready to fire the bricks.

It's worth noting that two beneficiaries have already begun the foundations on their plots.

CONSTRUCTION

Construction will be done using pre-cured bricks. That means that after pressing the bricks, we must wait several weeks before firing them and at least one or two weeks before using them for construction. Occasionally bricks break in the kilns, and the kilns themselves take several days to construct.

CONSTRUCTION MATERIALS

We rejoice in the fact that construction materials that left Boso-Djafo have already arrived at Bolomba and have been in The Fuller Center warehouse since July. We have sheet metal, nails, roofing nails, locks, hinges, and so forth. We got these to the warehouse thanks to the outboard motor which The Fuller Center bought for us in Kinshasa in order to help transport materials from Mbandaka to Bolomba. The outboard motor is in good condition and works well, as does the pirogue. The arrival of the materials delighted the beneficiaries, who hurried to the presses to make more bricks.

DIFFICULTIES/CHALLENGES

We face numerous challenges, among them:
The absence of a bank at Bolomba or Mbandaka

The absence of stores to purchase construction materials
Lack of road transportation
Nonpayment of government workers by the state
Shortage of fuel for the outboard motor
Rain at any time, etc....

OUR HOPES

The beneficiaries are pleased that more construction materials, for which the funds have already been received in Kinshasa, will support the continuation of work (seven other houses).

All in all, work at the site of FCH Bolomba is proceeding slowly but surely, despite the numerous challenges we face. We know that getting started is always the hardest part. We continue to educate the beneficiaries through counseling and seminars in order to keep them going.

The FCH Bolomba Board is also pleased that the visit of Mr. David Snell will take place in January 2009 and not before. By that time, we won't only have 2 or 3 houses but several more. The beneficiaries would prefer to have more houses finished before his arrival.

August 2009

I'm in Kinshasa staying at the CAP, which is a hotel of sorts run by the Presbyterians to provide affordable lodging to traveling ministerial types. It cost $50 a night for a very modest room and two meals. Breakfast was tea and bread with butter and jelly. There doesn't seem to be hot water. It's not unlike the UN station in Mbandaka except they serve good food. And the bath, as the Brits would say, is en-suite.

Things got off to an inauspicious start for this trip. I had to stop in Americus so I went through Atlanta. The flight was delayed by an hour due to thunderstorms there. Then we couldn't land and ended up in Huntsville for fuel. We finally got to Atlanta at about 6 o'clock, four hours late. Then the bags didn't come. They finally showed up on carousel nine and we'd been waiting dutifully at carousel three as instructed. By the time we got them I had missed the Columbus shuttle but was able to rent a car and get to Americus at 4:30 AM. I grabbed a couple hours of sleep, rearranged my bags, and left for Atlanta after a short stop at the Fuller family reunion.

The flight to Kinshasa was uneventful except I had to change planes at De Gaulle—one of my least favorite airports. So now I'm here. Maloka will pick me up soon for some meetings. We met with a number of folks from CONAFA (Congo North America Friendship Association), Pierre Maloka's organization working on improving lives in Congo, in Bolomba. They're working with a Canadian NGO that will provide a market for produce grown in Bolomba. I also met with a number of congressmen, two of them from *Equateur* Province. I spent a lot of time with them discussing our approach to charitable giving – they were very interested. One problem here, hard to believe, is an entitlement mentality. They were very intrigued by the concept of self help in dealing with the poverty mindset.

I'm in the airport in Kinshasa waiting for the flight to Mbandaka. Our delegation includes Maloka, his assistant Thomas, and the Honorable Josie Engabonda, of Equateur Province. We're flying Hewa Bora, which is always late. We go from here to Gemela then back down to Mbandaka. We left the CAP at seven and managed to get to the airport by 7:40 – a remarkable feat. We had a 10:30 flight that finally left at noon, getting us to Mbandaka at 3:00. Turned out that the governor's wife was on our plane so we had quite a reception. I got to see the governor, though, and get an invitation to dinner. They have an interesting greeting here—they touch foreheads three times, right, left, right, a greeting that the governor shared with me.

We settled into our lodging at the Rock of Ages Inn—not bad, en-suite but no hot water, a comfortable bed, and it comes with breakfast—tea (apparently there's no coffee in Mbandaka today) bread and an omelet. Dinner, late, at the governor's. He's providing the boat for the Bolomba trip. Things have improved since we first met. The first meal we had with him—a breakfast—was in a small official house with mismatched tableware. Now he's settling into his new digs—a much nicer place. Dinner there was a formal affair. We dined alfresco at more of a state event with new china, crystal and linens. As his fortune has improved so has Mbandaka's. The city is looking good, relatively speaking. Government buildings have been painted and the litter has been picked up. Dinner included rice, greens, (cooked like spinach), several types of fish wrapped in leaves and cooked over charcoal, an indeterminate meat dish, fried plantains and—get this—elephant, a special treat in my honor. The fish was good, the rice and greens marginal and the elephant sort of musty—a strange flavor similar to but not quite like mutton. It did break my heart to be eating elephant.

We got up early for a 7:30 meeting with the provincial congressional delegation from Kinshasa. The meeting started at nine. We talked Fuller Center philosophy. I'm learning that what is second nature to me—sharing, self-help, mutual help—has the quality of newness here.

We spent the day waiting to go to Bolomba. Literally the entire day. It turned out that Mbandaka had been without gasoline for two weeks but a new supply arrived yesterday. So getting the three barrels we needed for the trip turned out to be troublesome. By early afternoon they had secured the gasoline but had to transfer it from a 55-gallon drum to 5-gallon buckets. This was apparently proceeding well until the electric pump broke down so they had to finish the job with a hand pump. They finally showed up by late afternoon with 28 jugs of gasoline. By the time the boat was loaded it was dark so I made the decision to wait until dawn so we wouldn't be in danger on the river. We agreed to meet at 4:30 in the morning to begin the voyage and, like a good soldier, I was there on time. The rest of the crew showed up a little after five—all but one of the boatmen, who got in about 5:20.

We launched at 5:30 which worked well as the sun was coming up. We got to Bolomba at 9:15—record time—and got the day's events started. The proceedings included a fair amount of sitting and being looked at. First we had a town meeting where we were received by the assistant mayor. Then we went to the Catholic Church which is being rebuilt. It was in ruins when we were there on my first trip as a result of the civil war. We all sat in chairs lined up on the porch of the seminary building, where we had stayed on that first trip. It turns out this was simply a rest stop. I helped shorten it some as we had a set departure time of 3:00 and it was getting on towards noon. At 12:30 we made our way over to the building site.

I've been told that we were going to dedicate 10 completed houses. After we got to Mbandaka, Pierre, after visiting with Alemboa, told me that there were only six done and four started. When we got to the site I saw several unfinished houses and assumed the finished ones were down the road. We had a nice welcoming ceremony with more speeches held in one of the unfinished houses and then took off to start dedicating. It turned out there were no finished houses in Bolomba but five with roofs and one with trusses. I saw no evidence of the four that were under construction. It seems that when Alemboa told us that the houses were done he meant that the roofs were up. I was irritated.

We went ahead and dedicated the six. They're going to be nice homes—solid, handmade brick, and steel roofs. Apparently they had forgotten to address such issues as kitchens, latrines and floors, so we still have some work to do. The families, though, were great and very excited about having their own homes. I learned that there was some fear about the metal roofs and one man actually backed out of the program for fear that he would be killed because he had one. One of the problems with the project may be a carryover from Habitat days. Apparently, in order to cut costs, towards the end they made more and more demands of the homeowners. I kept hearing talk of how The Fuller Center provided the roof and the families had to build the walls so the houses are roofed but unfinished because most of the families, who work for the government, haven't been paid in six months and can't afford to pay masons. And our guys are afraid to spend money. One reason we never hear from them, despite the $1200 satellite phone we bought them, is because the usage charges are so high. We had quite a meeting when we got back to Mbandaka about next steps and communications.

We left the site a little before three and trekked to the church where they had a service in memory of Millard and Jim Conway, who passed away a week or so after Millard died. We got to the boat at 4:00. The trip home was uneventful. We sped down the Ikalemba until about 6:30 when the darkness settled in. It was slower going after that and a little anxious as we prayed to avoid pirogues and river bandits. About 45 minutes out of Mbandaka we got hung up on the sandbar but our crew was able to manhandle it free. We all breathed a sigh of relief when we could finally see the lights of the Rock of Ages pier, which is actually a couple of riverboats and pirogues anchored next to shore. We then had our come-to-Jesus meeting and got to bed about 11 o'clock.

We're heading back to Kinshasa on CAA Airlines this time. They told us to be at the airport at 6:00 AM for the 10:30 flight for reasons that are mysterious to me. Seasoned travelers on this run know that the 10:30 flight wouldn't leave until 11:30 at the earliest. A friend of the governor was traveling on our flight so we had the benefit of his intelligence sources. So we had a leisurely breakfast riverside — coffee, bread, and a can of sardines. We got word at about 10 o'clock that the plane had arrived so we made our way to the airport where we only had a short wait before boarding. I did have an unhappy moment on the tarmac. The DNG, (I don't know what that means but they're all over the airport) stopped me on the tarmac and made a fuss over my passport. I'm not sure what the problem was but it made for an uncomfortable few minutes. My expediter and the DNG guy yelled at each other for a few minutes. He then handed me back my passport and the expediter told me to run, so I did. Got back to CAP at 4:00 and called it an early day.

On Monday we headed back to Makana in the Republic of Congo. The trip over the river was a little harrowing. Pierre picked me up at about eight, then we picked up a TV reporter and had to take him to immigration to get his transfer document stamped. We got to the harbor a little before nine and went to the VIP waiting room, which was air-conditioned to the point of causing a chill. They took my passport and the others' papers and we sat, slowly freezing, until about 10:25 when they took us to the boat—without my passport so I was a little anxious. Finally, a guy showed up on the boat and passed out our papers and we were off. It was a 20-minute trip on a small ferry. When we got to the other side we went through an amazing bureaucratic process to get let back in. Everything got reviewed and recorded multiple times—not a computer terminal in sight. I finally ended up with a rather severe woman who recorded my information yet once again, gave me a nod and a stamp and we were on our way.

From there we went directly to Makana—an hour and a half trip over a hellish road that is as bad now as it was both of the other times I've been on it. Our party included Pierre and his assistant Thomas, the TV reporter, Gabriel, Christina and Edward from IHPD, and Landry from the embassy. Apparently the self-help model has hit a snag in Makana. The folks there feel they're too old to do the work and our folks, who aren't well-trained and are a little rigid, have been struggling with this. They want folks to toe the line but don't have a real sense of what that means. Christina has a schoolmarmish approach which, when coupled with her profound whiteness, is off-putting. Landry does much better but is still a little rigid, taking his marching orders from Christina.

We visited for a while and came to terms. I told them that if they wanted to pay for help to go for it but that we couldn't pay for it. We also learned that communications are weak even though they're only a cell phone call away so we agreed to work on that and stay better in touch with Landry being our point of contact and Edward as our backup. Maloka then spoke to the group and the effect was fascinating. The crowd was rapt – following his every word. He's agreed to help as well. I think we can salvage this. We then visited three of the four houses. Only one is done and looks very nice. One other is done except for doors and windows, the third needs floors, doors and windows, and the fourth, the chiefs house, has the walls up.

We stopped at Noura's in downtown Brazzaville for lunch and got back to the dock at 3:30. Then we got to experience yet one more episode of passport control. We cleared all right but when it came time to board the boat the expediter wouldn't give us the papers back because Thomas had apparently failed to pay some exit fee. They were starting to push the boat away and I stopped them saying that without my passport I wasn't leaving. I had one foot on the boat and one foot on the dock and there I stood in righteous indignation. Thomas came through with a last-minute payment. I got my passport and we were on our way. On the DRC side we got processed without any drama.

We came back to the CAP and met with a very interesting gentleman, Azarias Ruberwa. He's a former vice president and keeps an office here at CAP (the nicest interior space I was in the entire trip); he's sharp and very interested in our work. He'd like to get things started in South Kivu in the East. It would be a real boost to the program to have a man like this involved.

My last day in the Congo followed form. I spent a fair amount of time waiting and then had some good meetings. I saw the former vice president again and met with another deputy from Equateur. He ended up being very helpful letting us use his car and driver to get to the airport (for a small fee for gas—don't know how much he got but I contributed 8,000 francs). We left CAP at about 3:00 without much to do so we drove to a small fishing village a few miles beyond the airport. Apparently it's a weekend getaway site for Kinshasa folks. It was an experience. I've mostly been in places like Kinshasa, Mbandaka and Bolomba. This was something else entirely. We drove all the way down to the port. I'm looking for the words to describe it. Dirty isn't quite adequate. Overrun applies but doesn't capture it. It was teeming with people in a relatively small area. It was a market site with lots of basics for sale – plantains, tomatoes, manioc and all manner of fish live and recently live, whole chopped, dried, smoked. Also striking was the number of abandoned fishing boats. They were huge compared to the pirogues on the Ikalemba. Maloka had relatives there (he seems to have them everywhere) so we got to say hello any number of times.

We got back to the airport at about 5:00 with plenty of time to kill. We almost got into the VIP lounge but they wouldn't let Maloka's brother in (the two deputies and I made the cut) so we regrouped. Maloka's brother decided to wait in the car so we went back and this time they wouldn't let me in because I didn't have a diplomatic passport – apparently while we are regrouping the doorkeepers were as well. So we went back to the cars for a long wait and Thomas took my papers and got me through passport control without my having to be there—it's fascinating how things work here. We were waiting, in part, for John and Charity, Maloka's Canadian NGO friends, who were coming in from Paris on the plane that will take me back. The idea was that we could meet up in the interval. The plane was a little late, though, and Thomas and I were both anxious to be done with formalities, so we went on in to get me cleared through security. We almost made it when Maloka called to say that they showed up. It was too late for a meeting so once I got in the waiting room I gave them a call.

The last dramatic moment came when I got on the bus for the plane. They have an exit tax now—$50!—and you turn in the stub as you leave the airport building. They don't have signs telling you that your plane is boarding. Instead a woman stands at the door and shouts that the flight is ready. I got to the door, handed in my exit tax stub, and got on the bus to get to the plane. I asked a young man ahead of me if he lived in Paris and he said no he was from Brussels and was going home. Apparently I'd misunderstood the gate lady and was getting ready to board the wrong plane. I was able to get back to the terminal, retrieve my tax stub and wait for the call for the Paris flight.

August 13. 2011

I'm on the road again, this time back to Congo with a United Church of Christ Global Builders team. The UCC collaborates with the Disciples of Christ in its mission work, and it was the Disciples that sent Millard and Linda to Zaire almost 40 years ago. So this is a trip of historical import, a return to the place where Millard's house building vision turned from a notion into reality.

We'll spend a little time in Mbandaka on our way from Kinshasa to Bolomba. It was in Mbandaka that the first Partnership houses were built overseas. The story of this effort is told in Millard's first book, *Bokotola*, and a great tale it is. Our friend Don Mosley, who is working so hard on our North Korean initiative, did the survey work for that first community. This is a place rich in history.

The first houses were built on a parcel of vacant land in the heart of the city, a place called Bokotola. The area was barren because it marked the separation between where the white settlers and the black Congolese lived. On July 4, 1976, the day America was celebrating its bicentennial, the housing project was dedicated. 162 houses had been completed—and the waiting list had grown to over 5,000. At the dedication service Pastor Boyaka Inkomo, regional bishop of the

Disciples, spoke. In his concluding remarks he said, "We now propose to the authorities of the Sub-Region to change the name of Bokotola, which signifies 'the person who does not like others,' to Losanganya, which means 'reconciler, reunifier, everyone together'".

Now, some 35 years later, we are building again in Zaire, now called the Democratic Republic of Congo, in the village of Bolomba. Bolomba is in the deep jungle, some five hours by boat from Mbandaka. It is a place from the past, with no electricity, no television, no cell phones. It was also the site of one of the last battles in the 2001 civil war so, like so much of Congo, it is a place in need of reconciliation. It is a place of great poverty, but the people there, like people all over the world, seek a better life for their children. They laugh and love and share of what little they have with those who have less. We're off on a great adventure.

I'm at Dulles now waiting for my flight to Brussels then on to Kinshasa. Kirk Lyman-Barner, who works with our US covenant partners, is in the group along with Ryan Iafigliola, our Director of International Operations, and Craig Martindale from Kononia Farm and three from the UCC. The UCC group has been raising money to pay for a sawmill in Bolomba. This is a big group—can't wait to see how they take care of us there. My other trips have been groups of me and they've been logistically challenging.

Got to Kinshasa at about 8:00 PM and called Sheilla to learn that Glen Barton had died suddenly on Saturday night. This is a shock. Glen Barton's life exemplified sacrificial giving. Through his dedicated efforts, first in Shreveport and then as Director of U.S. Field Operations, Glen did more than anyone to establish The Fuller Center across the United States. He will be greatly missed as a fellow worker, a partner and a friend. I've been worried about him over the past year or so. He had kidney problems last winter and I believe that led to dialysis. He lost a lot of weight and never seemed to get his coloring back. Last month they gave him an aggressive treatment for a urinary tract infection that apparently had been hanging on for months. The word yesterday was that the infection has gotten into his heart. My first thought was that I should turn around and go home. Sheilla and the folks at the office didn't think so and I spoke to Brenda, Glen's widow, and she said to stay. They're having a funeral Saturday in Tallahassee. She said that a lot of the staff will go. They're bringing his ashes to Andersonville. If Brenda is all right with it we'll have a Fuller Center send-off then.

THE TATTERED PASSPORT

We spent the night at the CAP and are planning to leave at 9:00 in the morning to go to the airport but we got awakened at 5:30 with an urgent call to leave by six. We did and drove to the CAA airlines office where we were apparently set to do our paperwork, load a bus and be driven directly to the plane for an earlier departure. The bus was driving out as we drove in so we went ahead to the airport and sat there from 7:00 until 2:00 when the 1 o'clock flight finally took off. We got up to Mbandaka at 3:30 and out of the airport at 4:30. We came directly to the guesthouse, dropped off our stuff, and went to the home of the Disciples president for dinner.

We got up early for the trip to Bolomba. Now it's going on 3:00 in the afternoon. Our plan was to leave for Bolomba at 9:00 in the morning but apparently the truck needed repairs. It's too late now to leave and get there before dark so we've agreed to get up early and on the road tomorrow. We pretty much lost the day. We stayed at the guesthouse and watched the river flow by. We did get a short tour in the afternoon of Bokotola and Losanganya and bought some provisions. We had dinner at the Disciples president's house again—food that we brought this time.

We're traveling by car this time rather than by boat. They tell us that the road to Bolomba has been improved and that we should have a short trip. We loaded into a long-body Land Cruiser with facing bench seats in the back. All of us but one with the driver and his assistant/body guard for a total of 11. One of our members, Leah, opted to ride on the back of Benjamin's motorcycle. We got off to an inauspicious start when the jeep wouldn't fire up and had to be pushed. But we were soon on our way. We got stopped by the police in a small town south of Mbandaka—turns out that it was 6 o'clock and everything stops while they raise the flag.

We then drove, and drove, and drove. The road wasn't too bad most of the way but deteriorated the closer we got to Bolomba, narrowing to a bike trail. We had to stop from time to time to repair the bridges. We got a flat about an hour and a half in. We lost the motorcycle at that point – something that turned into the most serious challenge we would face. We passed through countless villages, all very much alike—a series of long narrow houses evenly spaced and facing the road. Some were adobe brick, some daub and wattle and a few cinderblock, all uniformly brown. Village life seems the same from early morning until evening—people sweeping their yards with palm fronds, kids running and yelling hello as we drove by, less dignified folks begging for money. There were lots of goats, chickens and

107

ducks and a few cows, all vying for space on the road. A few foul gave their all for our progress.

We stopped at a village for Maloka to do some politicking. We were given lunch and Pierre spoke to the crowd. Apparently they didn't like the message because it got pretty raucous. We fled to the Land Cruiser hoping for a quick escape. It wouldn't start. Suddenly the would-be rioters turned into good Samaritans and gave us a push and we were on our way. We had one other scary incident when a group of young men ran out of the jungle and jumped on the van. They were trying to untie the ropes that held our luggage to the roof. Our bodyguard sent them packing and we left them in the dust, or at least as much dust as one can raise at five miles per hour.

We finally got to Bolomba at four—an 11+ hour drive. The ferry was waiting but apparently broken down or out of gas so a motor pirogue pushed the entire rig across the river. This was actually our second ferry crossing of the day. We took a very nice boat across the Riku. I have memories of both ferries– I visited them with Pierre and Jim Conway on my first trip over. They had been taken by Bemba troops at the end of the last war so they could escape down the river. They ended up in Mbandaka where they were repaired and returned to service.

We hadn't seen Leah and Benjamin since the flat tire and were all concerned. They told us at the Riku ferry that they had seen a motorcycle with a white woman on the back cross the river on a pirogue so we felt better. But when we finally got to Bolomba we found that they hadn't arrived. At this point all of the quaintness of life in the Congo—awful roads, limited communications capability, dysfunctional services—was replaced by anger and frustration. We went through the welcoming ceremonies with a high-level of anxiety. We wanted to do something but there really wasn't that much that we could do. The ham radio was down, darkness was settling in so we couldn't really go after them. The last two hours of the road is just a track in some places—not something to tackle after dark. It was a long night. We managed to get some sleep but we were heavy-hearted. Congo is not a place to go missing.

Leah and Benjamin were still missing when we got up in the morning. We decided to take care of a little business and then head back towards Mbandaka to see if we could find them. The governor was in town and wanted me to join him to speak to the community. There was a good sized group and just as I was about to speak a motorcycle drove into the square with another following. Our errant sheep had finally rejoined the fold. It turned out that the bike had broken down just about the time we had our flat and they had returned to Mbandaka for repair. They got back on the road but when it got dark they stopped in a village and spent the night at the home of Dr. Diderot Bolingo, someone who would later play an important role in our work in Bolomba. With the lost now found we went on to enjoy a great day.

Because we lost a day in Mbandaka, we were only going to have the morning in Bolomba as we had to go back to catch our plane to Kinshasa—there are only a couple of flights a week. We had a lively ceremony at the building site and once again dedicated the still unfinished houses. I was given a live chicken and a stalk of bananas, which I donated back to the community. I wasn't sure how I'd get a live chicken through customs.

We got back in the jeep in the early afternoon with the assurance that the return trip would be much quicker, especially as we'd repaired all the bridges on our way in. We finally got to the outskirts of Mbandaka at 2:00 in the morning. I was able to get a signal and called Sheilla to let her know I was safe. She figured I'd been taken hostage by rampaging pygmies. The trip back to the States was uneventful. I doubt, though, that we'll be sending Global Builders teams to the Congo anytime soon.

March, 2014

Thursday afternoon and I'm back in Kinshasa—smooth entry this time. I'm here to meet with some of the leaders from Bolomba. We'll meet in Mbandaka so I won't be making the trip up the river. Pierre's assistant, Thomas, picked me up at the airport and took me to a Catholic retreat center where I was exiled for a day. It worked out well—I managed to get some sleep and do some writing. Tomorrow, Saturday, we'll fly up to Mbandaka.

It turned out that leaving Kinshasa was a lot more difficult than getting in! There was lots of paper shuffling but I made it through. I misjudged the boarding riot, though, so found myself well back in line. This is dangerous here as they load passengers until the plane is full and then close the door. More than once I've seen people standing on the tarmac wondering what happened. They were doing a second bag check on the tarmac, this for a flight going to Mbandaka, Gemena and back; probably not high-risk. They took my carry-on and loaded it with the checked baggage—not sure why. They loaded it all into a big box truck which they unloaded with great deliberation. I was able to watch from my seat and was happy to see my bag—the last one—loaded onto the plane. I noticed that the Hewa Bora booth in the terminal was empty. I asked about it and was told, "Oh, they crashed their last plane and had to go out of business." Air travel in Africa is an act of faith.

Sunday morning and it's time for church. We went with the Disciples of Christ and it was a great service. More singing than preaching. It was the Day of the Woman so the ladies ran the service. There were three choirs, all small but powerful. The first was all men and they provided the most fascinating choral rendition I've ever heard in a church house. They sang and danced—we could have been at a tribal celebration in a village deep in the jungle. Then there was a mixed choir—very strong—and finally a youth choir that may have been the church's nod to a contemporary service. The sermon was about self-help, having faith and getting busy. I couldn't have done better.

In the afternoon we went to Bolenge, the site of the Disciples' school and hospital complex. It was a little sad. Instead of restoring and maintaining these great old buildings, which will never fall down, they're letting them turn into a ghost town and putting up new buildings around them. I felt bad for Pierre, whose old high school is going to ruin.

On Monday we had good meetings with the teams from Mbandaka and Bolomba. Both groups want to get things moving and have strong leaders—Pr. Bonanga in Mbandaka and Dr. Bolingo in Bolomba. Pr. Bonanga is the DRC president of the Disciples of Christ and the host of a number of meals that we've had at his home. Dr. Bolingo has been recently assigned as the medical director in Bolomba. It was at his village home that our errant motorcyclists from the last trip found refuge. Both are busy men, but get-it-done types, so there is hope.

We then visited Bokotola. The owner of the first house there, who was the Fullers' cook, has passed away. We met another original owner, Papa Ikete, who lives there with his family still. Mbandaka was once a grand city—you can see it in the bones of the colonial buildings that survive. But it has gone into serious decline everywhere except for Bokotola, which stands as a testament to our philosophy of enlightened charity.

Tuesday was a quiet day—I think we've worn people out. I had a good meeting with the new governor, Gov. Impeto. He's a different sort from the last one; seems less worldly and a little more humble. We also signed the partnership covenant with the CDCC—the Disciples of Christ—for the work in Mbandaka and with the Pierre Maloka Foundation for Bolomba in French and English. We had a nice dedicatory service in the chapel at the Disciples headquarters.

110

That evening Dr. Bolingo took us to dinner at the Nina River Hotel, a rather nice place that I had never seen. I had a delicious meal of fish and French fries—a real treat. Then it was back to Kinshasa and then home.

EPILOGUE

I've had great hopes for our work in the Congo but things have never quite come together. This is one place that could benefit from a Habitat-style international partner, folks mostly from North America who lived in the communities overseas and helped manage the work. We haven't used them because we're more interested in developing strong local leadership. In a place as remote as Bolomba with communications so challenging and the absence of Fuller Center experienced leadership having someone on the ground who is well trained in our philosophy and practices may well be the way to go.

DAVID SNELL

DEMOCRATIC PEOPLE'S REPUBLIC OF KOREA

July, 2008

I am writing from Beijing after spending the last few days in Pyongyang, capital of the Democratic People's Republic of Korea, where I had meetings with officials to discuss the possibility of the Fuller Center starting work there. Our sessions were very fruitful and I hope to announce the start of a building project there soon.

This initiative will be considerably different from any we have undertaken and holds great promise for us to be part of the much needed effort at building trust and friendship between the people of the DPRK and the U.S. It could be another example of The Fuller Center serving as both a house building and a healing ministry.

Before I get into the details of our fascinating trip to the DPRK I thought I'd share with you a little about how it all came about. As you might imagine travel to North Korea doesn't just happen, and this trip wouldn't have been possible without the dedicated and patient work of two men, Dr. Han Park and Don Mosley.

Dr. Park is a professor of international affairs and the director of the Center for the Study of Global Issues (GLOBIS) at the University of Georgia in Athens. Dr. Park is trusted by both the U.S. and North Korean governments and, in the absence of formal diplomatic relations between our two countries, serves as a sort of ambassador-at-large. He has been a key player in many of the cultural and media exchanges we've had with the DPRK over the past 15 years.

Don Mosley lives just down the road from Athens in Comer, Georgia, at Jubilee Partners, a Christian community he co-founded in 1979, which has become a premier center for recently arrived international refugees. Don is well known as a peace activist, and has led peace making and humanitarian efforts in Nicaragua, the Middle East and Iraq. He was a driving force in the formation of Habitat for Humanity projects in Nicaragua, Lebanon and Jordan and is dedicated to the cause of peace through positive engagements. Don also served as a Peace Corps volunteer in South Korea.

Don and Han began working on this initiative over a year ago, and now, in God's good time, their efforts have borne fruit. We received invitations to come to North Korea in May and our team quickly came together. I had the privilege of traveling in distinguished company. In addition to Dr. Park and Don, our delegation included Kevin O'Donnell, Richard MacIntyre and Dr. Scott Adler. Kevin was the founding director of the Peace Corps in South Korea and served as Director of the entire Peace Corps in the early '70s. Richard is the Chairman of

MacIntyre Associates, a fundraising organization based in Kennett Square, PA. Dr. Adler is the Dean of the College of Agricultural and Environmental Sciences at the University of Georgia.

Monday, July 14: The first stop for Americans visiting North Korea is Beijing, which is where you get a visa and plane tickets. The process, though, begins much earlier. There is some tourism to North Korea primarily through authorized tour groups. Those traveling there to conduct business need to have their travel cleared in advance and receive an invitation from the appropriate state agency. Through the good efforts of Dr. Park we were invited and approved. The process was pretty straightforward—the embassy had the paperwork in order so all we needed were our passports, a visa photo and $100. We had an anxious moment when the officer told Han that he hadn't seen anything come through for him. The idea of making the trip without our mentor and guide was a little daunting. Turned out to be a little joke, and the visas were all issued without difficulty. The visa itself was on a separate card, so my passport shows no record of the trip. Alas. With our visas in hand we went to the DPRK state airline, Air Koryo, and $436 later had our tickets. We would leave for Pyongyang on Tuesday morning.

I need to say a word or two about Beijing. I really didn't know what to expect when I got there. Like most Americans, my impressions of the place were formed by what I'd seen in the media and were pretty much stuck in the 80s, when we saw the city as a drab, soviet-style place with avenues filled with bicycles. Things have changed. The Beijing we landed in is a thoroughly modern city of grand, architecturally interesting buildings, wide boulevards, lots of traffic, lots of greenery and lots of style.

I landed at Terminal 3, which is part of the massive new airport just completed in time for the Olympics. It's huge. But despite its vastness it's manageable and pretty friendly, although the security staff is a little testy.

Driving into the city one is struck by the quality of the freeway and the number of cars, but mostly how everything—the road, the cars, the buses—looks new. It's like the entire city just suddenly appeared, and to a certain extent I guess that's true. You get a peek into some of the older neighborhoods from the highway, so you know that the city didn't just suddenly materialize, but much of the city has been built, or rebuilt, over the last 10-20 years.

Tuesday, July 15: We got up early to get to the airport for our flight to Pyongyang. A little too early as it happened—we got to the airport at 9:00 for a noon flight. Fortunately, there was a Starbucks on the concourse. We were

114

anxious, though, and ready to get the next step taken. We'd gotten invited, picked up our visas and tickets, and now just wanted to be on the ground to be sure that this adventure was really about to happen.

We left Beijing at noon on Air Koryo flight 152. Our plane was a Russian Tupelov, fairly new and in nice condition. It's a short hour and a half flight, and you can imagine our surprise, being veterans of U.S. air travel, to have a full meal served in flight.

Pyongyang is an hour ahead of Beijing, so we arrived there at about 2:30 local time. There aren't many flights into Pyongyang so the airport was refreshingly calm. We were met by representatives of the Asia Pacific Peace Committee, who were our official hosts. The Committee was set up some years back to serve as a de-facto diplomatic outreach to countries with which the DPRK did not have diplomatic relations. They are very well connected and get high marks for making our trip both successful and pleasant.

We were escorted into a VIP lounge—very nice—where we went through passport control. Then down to pick up our baggage and go through customs. You go through security and x-ray both going into and coming out of the DPRK. I seem to have this Carlos the Jackal thing going for me as, once again in my life, I was the only one to have my baggage opened for review. The agent looked at my books and opened my ditty bag and then waved me through. They don't allow cell phones into the country, so those were confiscated to be returned, we were assured, on our departure. The whole entry process was easy and the officials were efficient and courteous.

Once out of the terminal we could finally say that we'd arrived. Until this point the trip was marked both by excitement and a certain anxiety. We were all stepping into something entirely new with no real understanding of what we would encounter. Our first half hour in North Korea, though, was calming, and would foreshadow the rest of the week. We were introduced to our guides, Mr. Che and Mr. Shin. These young men would be with us throughout the week, Chae serving as translator and Shin expediting all of our housing, feeding and travel arrangements. They turned out to be great companions and truly helpful to us during our stay. I made sure that Mr. Chae was never far from my side as I did my work—somehow speaking a little Spanish doesn't do you much good in the Far East!

From the airport to the hotel in the heart of the city is a 30-minute jaunt. The airport is in the countryside, and the fields were green and lush. We passed rice paddies and cornfields, interestingly juxtaposed. North Korea is hilly country with little flat, arable land, so every inch of good land is farmed. The country has gone through some difficult cycles of drought and flooding over the past few years, and food production is a primary national concern.

Pyongyang is a city of 2.3 million people and has been a capital city since the 10th century. It was almost entirely destroyed during the Korean War, so the city we visited had pretty much been built over the past 60 years. It's a city of broad avenues, monumental state architecture and apartment houses. There is very little private ownership of cars so traffic is light and is controlled by white-uniformed police, mostly young women, who stand in the center of the major intersections directing traffic with military precision. Their sharp, precise movements are like a martial ballet, and they are clearly not to be fooled with.

We were taken to the Koryo Hotel, one of a few hotels set aside for international guests. (Koryo is the name of one of the ancient kingdoms and present day Korea's name is derived from it.) The hotel is an impressive structure with twin, 44-story towers above the central area. I was on the 21st floor of tower 2, a great place to watch the rhythms of the city. It was built in the '70s and retains the flavor of what is now a bygone era. (I remember when we thought of the '40s as a bygone era. Time marches on.)

By this time our first day on the ground was drawing to a close. We had a great dinner in the hotel— *gujeolpan*, tiny pancakes with which small beef and vegetable burritos are made, and *bulgogi*, thin strips of beef, duck and squid barbequed at the table. Then off to bed to rest up for our first full day in country.

Wednesday, July 16: We awoke to a drizzly, overcast day, weather that was to pretty much accompany our entire stay. Our rooms at the Koryo Hotel included breakfast, so we found our way to the dining room, a bright, cheery, immense room that could easily double for affairs of state. There weren't many of us in the hotel this week, so our little group was pretty much swallowed up by the grandeur.

Breakfast began with a glass of yogurt, not the fruity confection we enjoy here, but something more along the lines of buttermilk. I'm sure it was good for us, but noticed that few of the glasses were empty at the end of the meal. We were then served coffee (in very small cups) and toast with the crusts cut off. There was a woman stationed in a corner of the room whose job it was to tend the toaster. We then had a torpedo shaped omelet—very good. The ritual was repeated every morning, and it provided a pleasant time for our group to reflect and plan.

At about 9:00 our hosts arrived, umbrellas in hand, to get us on our way. The first stop was the Mangyongdae Shrine on the outskirts of Pyongyang. This is the birthplace and childhood home of the Great Leader Kim Il Sung, a man who is revered in North Korea as the architect and builder of the DPRK. It was a fitting place to start our official time in the country. The shrine is set in a lovely park and centers on the family home. The Kims were tenant farmers, and Kim Il Sung left there in 1925 at the age of 13 to begin his personal struggle against the Japanese occupiers. Japan annexed the Korean Peninsula in 1910 and was an oppressive overlord. Their dominion ended in 1945, and Kim Il Sung returned to Mangyongdae to find that of all his family members only his grandmother remained—all the others had been lost in the conflict to free Korea.

The house is a small, thatch covered dwelling built around a central courtyard. It has been restored to the way it was in the early part of the 20th century. Among the visitors that day was a large troop of young soldiers. I'm afraid that some of them may have missed some of the tour—their attention was steadily directed at our little group of Americans. I hadn't felt like quite such an oddity since I was last in Bolomba,

We then went to the Paektusan Academy of Architecture, the government agency assigned to our project, and got down to business. The Academy is responsible for design and build projects, and much of the stately architecture of Pyongyang has come from their offices. We met with Mr. Sin, the Director of Foreign Affairs and Mr. Li, one of the Academy's architects. It was clear from the outset that our interests converged and the time we spent was fruitful.

In the afternoon we were taken to the Juche Tower, which honors the Juche Idea promoted by Kim Il Sung and further developed by Kim Jong Il. *Juche* is composed of two words, *Ju*, which means 'master', and *che*, which means 'oneself', so the philosophy is based on mastery of one's self. It is considerably more complicated than that and speaks to issues of independence and national self-reliance, born in part by a common will to never return to the subordination the country experienced under the Japanese. *Juche* has assumed the place of a national religion and no westerner can begin to understand North Korea without first trying to understand the tenets of *Juche*.

The Tower itself is some 560' tall and is topped with a red torch. It was built in 1982 to commemorate Kim Il Sung's 70th birthday, and is made up of 70 tiers. The number of stone blocks in the tower equals the number of days in 70 years. There is an observation tower at the top of the tower with 360° views of the city. Directly across the Taedong River from the tower is the majestic Grand People's Study House, a sort of national library, that stands on the west side of Kim Il Sung Square.

From the Juche Tower we visited the Arch of Triumph, a massive white granite structure that commemorates Kim Il Sung's leadership in the defeat of the Japanese, with the dates 1925 (when he left home) and 1945 (when the occupation ended) prominently featured. The Arch sits at the foot of the Moran Hills, which rise above the city and once protected its northern edge. We climbed to the top of one of the hills—a nice stroll for a group who had spent the last few days sitting in airports, airplanes, buses and meetings. Of course this was when the sun chose to poke out its head, so we were all glistening a little when we got back to the bus.

As our first full day in country came to an end we had a great Korean dinner at the hotel. I found the food in North Korea to be hearty, tasty and approachable. There were things on the menu that sounded a little daunting, but the fare I chose was consistently good.

Thursday, July 17, 2008—After our regular breakfast at the Koryo Hotel we went straight to the Academy to resume our discussions. What we're working on is significant, and will require both sides to dig deep. We'll have to adapt our model to meet the North Korean realities—there is no private ownership there, for example, so our homeownership approach won't fit. On their side the concepts of volunteerism and charitable giving are not well understood. But the remarkable thing is that Americans and North Koreans are sitting down to discuss ways of working together to get something good done. This could be how peace happens.

There's a lot left to work through, and decisions have to be made on both sides. But we are moving forward and left the meetings today feeling very positive. We broke for lunch and went to a small restaurant near the Academy for another delicious meal. We were introduced to *soju*, a vodka-like Korean liquor made of rice. It was served in shot glasses. After the toasts, and to the surprise of my hosts, I quaffed it down in a single slug. Apparently it's a sipping drink. They poured me another and, in the spirit of international cooperation, I sipped away. They drink it warm, but it would probably be great icy cold.

After a short break we were taken to the Manyongdae Children's Palace, a remarkable piece of architecture where children engage in a wide variety of extracurricular activities—music, sports, dance, *taekwondo* and who knows what else. The place is huge and is truly a palace, rich with marble, brass and chandeliers. We didn't know it at the time, but we were VIP guests for the weekly performance given by students of music and dance. We were ushered into the theater and given great seats, right next to the Cuban ambassador and in front of a group of 150 South Korean Christians who were in town, quite remarkably, for a church event.

The next hour and a half were filled with one spectacular performance after another. There were choirs, dancers, flautists, hoop acrobats, jump rope acrobats, accordionists, traditional musicians and a full orchestra (which was in the pit in front of the stage—I didn't realize that we weren't listening to recorded accompaniment until half-way through the show when I noticed the conductor's baton). The singing was outstanding, the instrumentals equally impressive and the dance numbers lovely. The kids, none of whom looked older than 14, were remarkably well rehearsed and looked like they were having a great time. Had the rest of our trip not been so productive that one event would have made the whole stay worthwhile.

Speaking of kids, North Korea is getting ready to celebrate its 60th birthday and in every square of any size we saw kids practicing for the event. Dressed alike in blue slacks, white shirts and red scarves, they were an impressive force. I'd like to be there when they all come together in September to show their stuff.

Friday, July 18: Our last full day in Korea started like the ones before it, with a breakfast of yogurt, toast and an omelet. We'd asked about the possibility of a site visit, so our counterparts from the Academy and leaders of the Asia Pacific Peace Committee took us into the countryside about 24 miles outside of Pyongyang. We visited three sites, all good candidates for a project. All are fallow farmland, all have power nearby, and all are close to existing villages from which the beneficiary families will be selected. Each will accommodate 50 to 75 houses with room for community facilities.

We continued our discussions about the project and I learned that they were concerned about both the scope and timing of our proposal. I had suggested that we consider building in 25 unit phases, which was misunderstood to mean no more than a 25 house project. I assured them that the initiative could be as large as funding would permit. I'd also suggested that we start building next spring, after the winter cold. They assured me that they were accustomed to working in the cold, and would like to start as quickly as possible.

North Korea is hilly and mountainous with relatively little good farmland. The area we visited is relatively flat, and farm work was in high gear. Workers were in the fields, cultivating, irrigating and harvesting. There were vast fields of cabbage, an essential for *kim chee*. We saw rice paddies and corn fields and the landscape was deep green as far as we could see. But the limited available farmland, coupled with massive flooding and crippling droughts over the past few years, has seriously impacted the country's ability to feed itself. There are concerns that this year's famine will be even worse than those of the past few years. Korea will need the world's help this year. Hopefully we'll put a little less grain in our gas tanks and be able to send a little more there to help feed a nation in need.

We agreed to continue our discussions during a follow-up visit in September. This would give them time to work on some plans and allow us to assemble a small team of professionals who could help deal with the issues of green building, alternative energy, water and sewer handling and heating. The latter is especially interesting as the traditional Korean heating system involves moving heated air, essentially stove smoke, through under-floor ductwork. It's not an environmentally friendly system and actually results in carbon monoxide deaths across the peninsula each winter. But the local folks aren't sure their houses are well heated if the floors aren't warm, so we will have to be creative with this one.

That evening we signed a Memorandum of Understanding between the Academy and The Fuller Center which will help guide our next steps and memorialize what we've agreed to so far. We're not ready to make a formal announcement about our developing partnership just yet, but

we have established a high level of understanding and trust and are confident that this initiative will move forward.

We ended the day with a spectacular meal at the revolving restaurant atop the Koryo hotel. The food was outstanding—this will be one of my more memorable dining experiences. Among the treats were sautéed pine mushrooms, a highly prized delicacy that would otherwise be beyond my means. We toasted our successful week, shared gifts, and talked about what was to come. It was a delightful end to an amazing adventure. Tomorrow we return to Beijing, and then on to the best part of any trip—going home.

I did have a moment of concern that evening. I was digging through my backpack and came across my Colorado cell phone. I didn't realize that I'd left it there. I figured that this was it, there'd be a midnight knock on the door and I'd be taken away. I guess that the maids never found it when they were cleaning my room and apparently I had my back to the giant mirrors that I figured someone was behind, watching when I pulled it out. Not that I'm paranoid, but we are talking North Korea here. I was able to smuggle the phone back out of the country, but now that I've told this story I probably won't get invited back.

Monday, December 15, 2008

I'm in Beijing today, getting things in place for a return trip to North Korea. We've been invited back to continue discussions on the house building initiative there. I spent the morning getting my visa and Air Koryo tickets. I leave tomorrow for Pyongyang and will be there until Saturday.

I'm soloing this time and getting the visa and tickets turned out to be an adventure. Last time we were with mentor Han Park who knows the ropes. The first challenge was finding the North Korean Embassy. I checked with the concierge at the hotel but English really is a foreign language here, and the address he came up with turned out to be for the South Korean embassy. Fortunately, I had my phone and a number and the taxi driver was able to figure it out. They had cards for Air Koryo at the embassy, so we were able to find that without too much difficulty.

Everything is now arranged and I'll be on the 11:30 flight tomorrow for Pyongyang. I won't be able to post to the blog while I'm there—no internet access—but will keep a daily record and put some thoughts down when I return.

This will be an important series of meetings. On the last trip we came to a general understanding on the project. This trip will begin to put some meat on the bones, talking about construction systems, materials, location, infrastructure and all the elements that will go into building a budget. One of the goals is to build houses that are highly efficient and innovative in terms of energy use. We could be on to something very interesting with this.

Tuesday, December 16, 2008 I was met at the airport by Mr. Che, who was our translator on the last trip and will be on this one as well, and Mr. Sin, Director of Foreign Affairs of the Paektusan Academy of Architecture, with whom I signed the memorandum of understanding on the last trip. They will be my companions for the week.

We rode in a government Mercedes. The first number of the license plate indicates the relative status of the riders. Ours had a seven, not at the top of the heap but sufficiently high to get us some respect. The traffic guards held traffic to waive us through and some of the troops, which are everywhere, saluted. In my overcoat and black hat I imagine I looked like some sort of Soviet apparatchik

I'm writing from the Koryo Hotel in central Pyongyang. This is one of the hotels designated for foreigners and my fellow travelers include World Food Program staff, nuclear compliance observers and others of undetermined provenance. Most of us seem to be Americans. The Koryo is a grand old hotel. The heat works, the water's hot, the food is good and the bed is comfortable enough to give me a good night's sleep. Not a bad place to spend some time.

Wednesday, December 17, 2008 Our first work day and we spent the morning going over a list of topics that I'd sent for discussion. Our conversation was wide ranging, but the heart of the issue is designing a community that is essentially self-reliant in terms of energy, water and sanitation, and is environmentally friendly in the process. No small order. We have a great opportunity here to do something that is cutting edge and replicable. What we do in North Korea could have implications for projects around the world.

We attended a performance of the State Symphony Orchestra in the evening—spectacular. There were two dozen violins and a dozen each of violas and basses. Interestingly all of the musicians except for two harpists were men. The program opened with a piano concerto that was dazzling. After that performance the stage under the piano descended and the orchestra played on. It was held in the Moranbong Theater, which overlooks Moran Hill. It could be the prettiest building in Pyongyang—not large, but well proportioned. Maybe it's because of its Greek style that speaks to my Western sensibilities. Asia seems to be working hard to preserve the classical music of the West.

We came back to the Koryo hotel for a working dinner. I haven't had a bad meal since I've been here. They tell me that the harvest was good this year and that, along with international support, has relieved the food crisis. There are a number of white Toyota 4X4s parked at the hotel that belong to the World Food Program. USAID is involved as well—a good sign.

Thursday December 18, 2008—We drove into the countryside today, about an hour south of Pyongyang, to a collective farm of some 1700 members who work 900 hectares (about 2,200 acres), mostly rice. The farm has been visited a number of times over the years by both leaders—Kim Jung Il was there just last week, which pretty much means he's up and around and Kim Il Sung visited a number of times. We toured the museum they've built to commemorate the Leaders' visits and then got to visit three homes. This was something I was anxious to do—it's one thing to look at pictures and house plans, but nothing beats getting into the actual home.

The houses were similar. They're small, less than 1,000 square feet—and each had two or three common rooms and a kitchen. There was very little furniture—Koreans spend their leisure and sleeping time on the floor. Each was neat as a pin. The kitchen configuration is different from any I've seen. Each had three or four wide, shallow pots sunk into recesses in the floor. In front of the 'stove' the floor planking was loose to allow access to the fire chamber below. One of the houses cooked over wood and straw and the other two over coal. Each of the kitchens had a small methane burner that burned fuel manufactured on site from the output of the latrine and pig sty.

One of the houses was off the grid completely and relied on a small wind generator for power. There was a large battery in the house to store the power made when the wind blows. The other two houses were on the grid but kept a battery charged for outages.

Behind each house, separated by a narrow walkway, was a row of outbuildings to house rabbits and pigs and for storage. At the last house we visited there were six pots buried to their necks in the ground—sure enough, it was the *kim chee* supply fermenting for the next season. Kim has mandated that every house in the country plant fruit trees, and every garden had a few. During his recent visit Kim expressed concern about some rabbits whose hutch was exposed and the house was redesigned to allow for an indoor space for the little guys.

There is no private land ownership in the DPRK, which stretches our homeownership model. There is, though, a manner of land tenure in that a tenant typically has a lifetime right of occupancy that can be transferred to the next generation.

Everyone I met on this trip was gracious and welcoming. I'm sure they'd been prepared for the visit. They probably don't know who I might be, but there was no question that I was a welcome guest. My travel was less restricted this time with trips into the countryside and through the back streets of Pyongyang. The more I travel the more I find that there is little that really separates us. We speak different languages and eat different foods, but there is an undeniable sense of brotherhood among us human beings that seeks friendship. This is something that happens at the individual level, but somehow gets lost when we deal with each other as groups and as nations.

Saturday, December 20, 2008 On my way home. It snowed last night—not much, just a few inches. People were mobilized to clear the streets. All along the highway to the airport they were moving snow with broad, wooden shovels. The airport terminal, like many public buildings, wasn't heated and the plane was late in leaving. I thought I might perish from the cold right there in the waiting room.

November, 2009

I'm back in the USA after a whirlwind of travel. From the Philippines I traveled to Beijing, the jumping off point for Americans traveling to North Korea, which was my destination. I was only in Korea for a couple of days, but they were momentous ones. I tried to post a blog when I got back to Beijing from Pyongyang, but apparently China and Google are having a tiff so I couldn't get into the program. I left China for Peru where we dedicated the first 20 houses, and then back here to Americus.

This was my third trip to the DPRK. With each journey I become more convinced that if people ran the world instead of politicians we might be able to live in peace. The North Koreans have a world view that is vastly different from ours and that difference has resulted in our pretty much being mad at each other for the last 60 years. But the Korean people, like people everywhere, are just like you and me. And at the grass roots level they just want to be friends.

On this trip I traveled with our board chair, LeRoy Troyer, Don Mosley, founder of Jubilee Partners and long-time Habitat and Fuller Center supporter, and Dr. Han Park, professor of political science at the University of Georgia and founder of the Center for the Study of Global Issues (GLOBIS). These visits to North Korea are the result of conversations Don Mosley and Han Park started over two years ago.

We didn't do much touring on this trip. We did visit the Mansudae Grand Monument with its 66-foot-tall bronze statue of Kim Il Sung, where I placed flowers at the base of the statue. This is a place of reverence in North Korea and we were expected to pay homage to the Eternal President.

I've had the opportunity of meeting with government officials, working people and farmers on my travels there. To a person they have been polite, friendly and interesting. Despite the many things we could probably find to disagree on there is one thought that we all share—it's time to come together.

But the big event, and the reason for this trip, was to break ground on The Fuller Center's first housing project in North Korea. We met with officials from our partner agency, the Paektusan Academy of Architecture, our hosts, the Asia Pacific Peace Committee, government

officials and local farmers at Osun-Ri in the Sunan District just outside of Pyongyang. We arrived to find the site partially excavated with house sites laid out. There were about 75 people at the site, farmers who will occupy the new houses. There was a long table with a welcoming banner and a podium on one end. We took our places behind the table and the program began.

There were a few speeches including mine, in which I spoke of the opportunity this project offers for Koreans and Americans to come together for a common good. I'm not sure how much of my speech was accurately translated. After the speech making about a dozen of us were given white gloves and a shovel. We lined up along one of the foundation lines and on cue all turned the soil, marking the beginning of what will surely be an incredible journey. After that we had the rare opportunity of mingling with the locals. The language barrier made a meaningful exchange difficult—Koreans don't like for visitors to speak the language and I'm told that they will deny a visa to a known Korean speaker. Nonetheless it was quite something to mingle openly with these farmers and to share their excitement at having new homes.

We returned to Pyongyang where we continued our meetings with officials of the Academy and signed an addendum to the memorandum of understanding that we'd signed on our first trip—a formal affair. We left the next day for Beijing.

September 17, 2010

It's been a gloomy day here in Beijing—warm but overcast and drizzly. This is the jumping off point for Americans traveling to the DPRK. We have to stop here to get a visa and pick up plane tickets for the trip to Pyongyang, which I spent the better part of the morning getting done. I actually spent very little time on the visa and tickets and a lot of time getting there and back.

I read somewhere that there are more Chinese studying English than there are people in the United States. If my experience is a teacher it's not going particularly well. Communicating is incredibly difficult here, and getting around can be quite the challenge.

I finally got to the embassy okay—I had the concierge write down the address for the cab driver. Unfortunately he gave the address for the South Korean embassy, but a guard there set us straight. Getting to the airline office was a little more difficult. It's in the Swissotel, but I couldn't seem to communicate that. First I couldn't find a cab so I ended up in a motorized pedicab with a driver who assured me he knew the way. We ended up at the Silk Market. Apparently Swissotel and Silk Market sound the same when said in English.

I found another cab and had the driver get the address from my hotel clerk— thank goodness for cell phones or I might still be wandering the streets. I got my tickets and found my way back to the hotel, soggy and a little weary.

Now things are in order for my travel to Pyongyang. I'll fly over tomorrow and will be there through Thursday of next week. This is an important series of meetings that will hopefully finalize plans for our house building work. A fundamental piece of this initiative is our agreement for volunteers from the States to join with Koreans to do some good. We hope to build peace, one house at a time, starting this fall.

September 19, 2010

I arrived in Pyongyang Saturday afternoon and was met at the airport by Mr. Sin from the Paektusan Academy and my interpreter, Mrs. Kim. My seatmate for the flight was a young man from Alberta, Canada, who was traveling with his wife and two sons and 11 other Canadians who are coming to Pyongyang to teach English for three months. This is one of the few cases I'm aware of where a longer stay is being allowed for western visitors. It probably helps that they're Canadians, but things seem to be changing in the Democratic People's Republic. At the airport I happened to meet the British Ambassador and the Hong Kong representative of the ATPN news group—a providential meeting perhaps.

On the drive into the city I noticed some change. There are massive renovation projects going on—the Cultural Hall and the National Theater are both being redone. The Academy of Architecture building is as well, which means that our working meetings will be here at the Koryo Hotel. Traffic lights have been installed and there are fewer of the blue and white clad traffic directors on the streets. The street that the Koryo sits on has been redone with new shops, neon signs, street lights and grass. I'm not sure what's going on, but the improvements belie the prevailing notions about the economic condition of the country.

I went to services today at the Bongsu Church. Pastor Son and the congregation greeted our little group of Americans warmly—I went with a delegation of doctors from Florida who are here doing heart surgery. It's a Protestant church, one of two here in Pyongyang. There's also a Catholic and possibly an Orthodox one as well. Freedom of religion is a right but there are very few active believers. I'm told that Christianity flourished here in the North before the communists took over and that a number of the successful evangelists in the South were from this side of the border.

The service was lovely. The choir was powerful. The sermon dealt with trust and faith taken from the reading in Romans 14: 22-23. They had simultaneous translation so we were able to follow along. There were some English hymnals, but I wasn't close enough to one to do more than hum. The closing hymn, though, was *God Be with You 'til We Meet Again*, one of my favorites so I sang lustily as we marched down the aisle to the front porch. Then the members left by the side door, and a very interesting thing happened that told me that maybe there really was some sincerity in all of this. Everybody in North Korea has a pin that they wear over their heart. It used to be a picture of Kim Il-Sung, but then it became both Kim Il-Sung and Kim Jong Il. Everybody has one. I tried to get one, but they told me no. When they left the church, I saw people putting their pins back on. So, they took their pins off to go to church. I might be reading too much into it but that seemed to indicate to me that there might have been some sincerity. There are only two or three churches in Pyongyang, and they've done a very effective job of promoting atheism there. But, nonetheless, there is a spark of belief.

September 20-22, 2010

We've had a very busy week here, dominated by meetings with our partner organization, the Paektusan Academy of Architecture. We are finalizing plans to get the construction underway. It's been a long time coming, but I think that we are close to getting some actual work done.

On Monday we visited Mangyongdae, the birthplace and childhood home of Kim Il Sung. His grandparents were farmers. Kim, his parents and siblings all went to China to fight the Japanese occupation—only Kim and his grandmother survived. We also visited the West Sea Barrage, a huge complex of levees, dams and locks that separate the Taedong River from the ocean, keeping sea water out of the lower river basin so that the fresh water can be used for agriculture. It was a monumental undertaking and was built in five years by some 40,000 soldiers. They took me there to demonstrate their construction capabilities—turned out to be foreshadowing, but I didn't recognize it at the time.

Our most important trip of the day was to Osan-Ri to visit the building site. There are 200 families living on the collective, and as a result of our work building 50 houses in addition to a government project to build another 150, all of them will have a new and decent home sometime next year. We're building on a tree nursery collective that provides tree stock to a large part of the country.

A final stop for the day was the E-Library at Kim Il Sung University. This was a project of the Paektusan Academy and took one of the original campus buildings and turned it into a state of the art computer center. Students can do research 'online' accessing thousands of books on terminals in a number of study rooms. Very impressive.

Monday evening was set aside for a special treat—we went to the *Arirang* mass games performance. This is an annual event that involves some 20,000 dancers and

128

gymnasts. The back bleachers are a solid mass of placard-bearing youngsters who change their cards to create panoramas that provide the backdrop for the performances. It was an amazing experience. I was exhausted by the time it was over just from watching.

On Tuesday we broke from our discussions to visit the Taedonggang fruit farm, a massive sea of apple trees that has grown from nothing to 1,600 acres since 2008. Big is a part of the culture here. We went to see some new houses that the Academy has been working on—very nice, very tidy and appropriate to what we will be doing.

Wednesday was a holiday—*Chusok*—when people take food made from the first fruits of the harvest to their ancestors' gravesites. We had a short meeting in the morning, but in deference to the holiday broke early so that Mr. Sin from the Academy and my very able interpreter, Mrs. Kim, could be with their families.

The final event was a meeting at the Koryo hotel with Mr. Sin and his superiors. The meeting was to lay the groundwork for the demands that they would soon be making and was unpleasant. They were not kind in their assessment of how the project was going and told me that if we would just send the money they could get the job done. I was told that Kim Jung Il has visited the site and taken a personal interest in it. If this is so that probably accounts for their more aggressive behavior. This was my first encounter with the darker side of negotiating and, for the first time in all my travels here I was anxious to leave the country.

December 10, 2011

Currently we have blocks on the ground at Osan-Ri to build three duplex units. We have purchased another duplex, which is in Beijing, and have paid for the manufacture of six more duplexes, which are also in Beijing. We do not have materials for anything more than the exterior walls for these units.

Our first work team arrived in Pyongyang in early December. It was not a successful trip. The team was held in Beijing for over a week awaiting visa clearance and ended up with only three days in Pyongyang. During that time they visited the worksite once and were allowed to put up a demonstration wall of block. Most of their time was spent in meetings being lectured by Academy leaders about our failures.

During those meetings the Academy demanded that we ship all of the materials to Osan-Ri by the end of March and send some $800,000 in cash over the next few months for them to use to complete the houses. If these demands stand they will result in the end of this partnership. From the beginning the idea of having American volunteers come into the country to work along with Koreans has been only modestly embraced by the Koreans. These demands indicate that that idea has met a dead end.

The week after our team returned to the States Kim Jong Il, leader of the country since 1994, died of a reported heart attack. His third son, Kim Jong Un, has been named successor. We hope that the transition is peaceful and opens even more doors to opportunities for peace and engagement with other nations.

For now, The Fuller Center for Housing is waiting until the transition of power has been finalized and we have had a chance to review the situation's potential impact on our mission there before proceeding further. We hope that the new leadership will embrace a relationship with The Fuller Center as an opportunity to help people move into safe and decent housing while establishing relationships that can lead to a more peaceful world.

March 6, 2012 STATEMENT ON NORTH KOREA BY FULLER CENTER FOR HOUSING PRESIDENT DAVID SNELL:

Some four years ago The Fuller Center for Housing was presented with the idea of building peace by building houses in North Korea. Our extensive experience in challenging locations, places like the mountains of Peru, the jungles of the Congo and the Himalayan foothills of Nepal, made us a likely partner in such an effort.

We were most taken with the possibility this project offered for Americans and North Koreans to come together in a common cause and get to know one another as brothers and sisters rather than historic enemies. Those of us who have had the good fortune of traveling to North Korea can attest to the warmth and friendship that was shown to us.

Over time, however, the challenges of logistics and communications have overtaken the initiative, and it is with sadness that we announce its indefinite suspension. Perhaps the future will bring new opportunities for efforts like this to proceed, but for now we must step back.

We continue to wait prayerfully for the day when all of God's people can come together in peace. Our experiences in North Korea confirm what we've learned around the world, that despite the apparent differences that separate us we are all pretty much alike, sharing the dream of a better world for our children.

130

August 9, 2017

The following is an interview I had with the Fuller Center's Communications Director, Chris Johnson, about our experience with the Democratic Peoples' Republic of Korea:

How did this Fuller Center project in North Korea begin?

This all started when our friend Don Mosley from Jubilee Partners, who'd been involved with Millard since Mbandaka (where the Fullers worked in then-Zaire 1973-76) came to us. He'd made friends with Dr. Han Park at the University of Georgia. Dr. Park was well-connected with both North Korea and U.S. leaders and was able to navigate between the two. They came up with the idea of The Fuller Center building some houses in North Korea. The idea was that we would fund them, but we'd work with the North Koreans to design them.

The key to it was we'd send U.S. volunteers over to work with the Koreans in getting the houses built. The idea was — as we stated in the memorandum of understanding we signed in Pyongyang — that it might "foster friendship and trust between all persons involved."

So Dr. Park arranged for a small group of us to travel over to North Korea, and we met with officials at the Paektusan Academy of Architecture, who were going to carry the ball on the Korean side. We started talking about it, and it sounded like a pretty good idea.

Did you get any pushback against this idea of working with North Koreans?

Actually, very little. We had one donor who wrote and said he'd never give us another dime because we were "cavorting with the enemy," but that was the only real visible objection. I'm sure there were people who were concerned, but that was the only actual resistance we got.

What was the actual housing plan for Osan-Ri?

They initially wanted us to build in Pyongyang, but everything in Pyongyang is huge, very expensive condominium-style apartments and housing blocks. We said no, that we would build in the country where we're comfortable and we'll build single-family homes. So we ended up in Osan-Ri and were going to build 50 houses there. It was a tree farm as I recall. Some of the housing was derelict and needed to be replaced. Then the Koreans were going to continue the project and build another 150 houses.

You knew how tough this would be. Why even try?

If you don't try, you know your result will be failure. And in the early days it was actually very encouraging. The folks in Korea were embracing of the notion by all appearances. I met some wonderful people there. The idea of doing something collaboratively like this would demonstrate both to Koreans and to Americans that we're not all that different and that although our governments don't agree on things, we can get along. So there was real momentum in the early days — on both sides — to do this.

What got in the way of that early momentum?

Well, we had some disagreement over the house plan itself. I visited a number of rural communities in North Korea and visited the homes there. They were really quite lovely homes — small but lovely two- and three-room homes. But they seemed well-built and were comfortable. So we were trying to design something that would accommodate that. There was some back and forth on what the actual house design would be.

There also was the building system itself. We were prepared to introduce a new system there. It's cold in North Korea and they used asbestos panels for insulation. We were suggesting a sort of Styrofoam block kind of system that we could bring in from China. They were actually kind of excited about that. We ended up bringing some of those blocks into the country.

It got worse and worse. I think what really happened was that in the early days they expressed excitement about the volunteers coming in. But as this thing progressed and it looked like something might actually happen, they weren't so sure they wanted that feature. It finally ended when they said, "We can do this. Just send us the money and we'll build the houses." That flew in the face of everything we were trying to do. The volunteer piece was fundamental to it. When that started to go away, then it appeared that we might not be able to do this.

In December of 2011, we sent a team of six Fuller Center volunteers to check on the project. A few days later, leader Kim Jong Il died. What were your hopes for the project and the country itself at that point of transition to the current leader, Kim Jong Un?

Things went pretty well when Kim Jong Il was in power there. He actually visited our site and had eyes on the project which made it more difficult for the Koreans because they were under the gun. When he died and the son took over, we were hopeful. (Kim Jong Un) was Western-educated, and maybe he'd bring new eyes and a new approach. It hasn't turned out to be that way. I'm actually thankful every day that we aren't sending volunteers to North Korea because things certainly changed, but not for the better.

What were your impressions of the country and the people from your four trips there?

I came to believe that what we know about them and what they know about us is mutually flawed. Pyongyang is not a bad-looking town. It's full of skyscrapers, and that's where everyone lives. That's the place to be in North Korea. I did get into the countryside, and I did visit with the folks. I know that they're carefully selected and things are orchestrated, but we had a groundbreaking at Osan-Ri with officials there with a long table and banners and got to speak and then we got to mingle with some of the farmers afterward. You know, they're folks just like us.

They have a whole different life. They're totally isolated. There's no information coming in. There are three TV stations and they all play the same thing — it's all propaganda. And they're taught from an early age that we are the enemy, America is the enemy, and that our goal is the destruction of North Korea. Regime stability is probably the most important thing for the government there. They watched their neighbors and what happened in the Soviet Union when Western influences started to show up and Western TV and movies came and they couldn't support that socialist system any longer. So they're keeping it out, and they're very effective at it.

I found that the food was delicious. I did not see starvation on a mass scale. Like I say, I can only report on what I saw, but I saw a fair amount.

Is it true that you went to church in North Korea?

I went to church. Again, people say it's staged but it seemed like there was a lot of sincerity in there. It was sort of a Presbyterian-style service. The choir was magnificent. They seated the guests up front, and we had headphones so we could pay attention to the sermon. There were a couple of times that the headphones went blank, so I figured the pastor must have been saying something they didn't want us to hear. At the end of the service, they walked us down the aisle, and the choir sang "God Be With You 'Til We Meet Again." It was very powerful.

We like to tout The Fuller Center's success stories, like the record building year we just had. How does this non-success story of North Korea fit into the annals of The Fuller Center?

It fits just where it ought to. It was certainly not a success in many ways — in any way, actually. But it was an education. We tried something. We're talking about a global thing. I realized when I was over there that we weren't dealing with peers. We were negotiating with the government of North Korea. But if you don't try, you know you're going to fail. We tried. We were blessed in that it didn't happen because it'd be a terrible thing right now. It's not a good time to be an American visiting North Korea. The volunteer component would have crumbled anyway. But you learn from your failures.

Now, I don't know anywhere in the world we could go that would be as challenging as North Korea. Cuba would be a cakewalk compared to North Korea. But we reached out and actually made some relationships. They can't sustain themselves because we can't communicate with them. And we don't know what we left behind. We don't know whose lives we may have touched. We'll never know, but, by golly, we made the effort.

With all the tension between the U.S. and North Korea today, do your experiences there put a human face on this political turmoil?

It does for me. I know some of these folks now. I've met them. One of the men that I worked with there I really enjoyed, just a wonderful guy, was in the equivalent of our State Department. Recently he was posted in New York at the United Nations. There's no way I could call him up and say, "Hey, how are things?" But he was a very decent man, and I wonder what's going through his head as we're watching all of this happen.

There's an interesting bunch there. When you arrive in North Korea, you're met by your translator, who is with you the entire time. You don't leave the hotel without them. It's their monitoring system; I'm not naive to that. But a couple of these guys were very interesting young men. They're exposed to the West. One of them came to me — in the upper floors of the hotel where the tourists stay, they had BBC and China TV in addition to the local stations — and he came to me and said, "Do you have BBC up there in your room" I said yeah. He said, "Can I come up and watch the news?" I said, "It's fine with me; I don't know about your folks." It was a 20-minute show that came on at five o'clock. He knocks on the door at five o'clock, I let him in and he came and sat five feet in front of that TV set, absolutely riveted for the entire broadcast. When it was done, he thanked me and left.

But there's a corps of these folks, a fair number of them, because every foreign visitor has someone to accompany them. I think at some point this is gonna fail; this regime can't sustain itself. And when that happens, I think these people are going to be in an interesting position to help guide the future. I was very taken with their intellect, friendliness and interest.

We've shared a photo gallery of just some of the images you've captured in North Korea. How did you bring home so many images?

I see these things on Facebook — photos that the North Koreans don't want you to see that some guy is secretly taking — I took pictures the whole time I was there. One place we went when we were first looking for a site out in the country, we could see in the distance artillery covered in camouflage. I thought, hmm, we might have gotten too close to that particular post. But I never had a problem and didn't have a problem getting my camera out of the country. So, I don't know. We blow things up in the West. One of the things that always bugged me is how Kim Jong Il portrayed as a buffoon in the American media. He wasn't a buffoon. He was an autocrat. He was a dictator. He was cruel. But he wasn't a buffoon. Now this youngster (Kim Jong Un), I'm not so sure about.

One thing I've learned from this and my other travels is if we could get governments out of the picture, we could probably all get along. Koreans, really, on a 1-to-1 basis, love to get to know folks. And that's true all around the world. If we could get governments out of the picture, we could probably have peace.

DPRK EPILOGUE & REFLECTIONS

When we first started talking about a trip to North Korea my expectations were low and my anxieties were high. Everything I knew about the country I'd learned from the media and a few books I'd picked up, mostly written by American writers. So everything I knew was, predictably, less than favorable. I committed to going with an open mind and to limiting any observations I might make about the country to my own experiences.

From our first introductions at the airport until we boarded the plane for home the interpersonal experiences I had were uniformly positive. Customs and passport control were no more onerous than in any other county I've visited, and actually easier than in some. Our companions for the trip were courteous and helpful and willing to answer any questions we had. We weren't allowed to wander on our own, but I don't do a lot of that wherever I travel, so that wasn't hard to bear. We couldn't bring our cell phones into the country, but we were able to take pictures of anything we chose.

The differences between the DPRK and the U.S. in terms of government, economy, culture and world view are significant. Our approach through the years has been to focus on those differences at the expense of finding those things we share. From my experience we share a great deal—a desire for a better life for our children, for security, for enough food to eat and a decent place to lay our heads when the day is done. But we also share, on a personal level, the desire to get along, to share a joke, and to accomplish something we feel good about.

North Korea is a country in need of friends. The collapse of the Soviet Union and the capitalization of China have left it with few partners on which it can rely. The economy is suffering and food production has been severely damaged in recent years by flood and drought resulting in near famine conditions. I saw no overweight North Koreans. Solving the food crisis will surely require that North Korea expand its international relationships. To borrow from John Donne, no *country* is an island. But the political philosophy that guides the North Korean government makes it difficult for it to reach out. Making a place for organizations like ours may be a way of inviting new friends into their camp. Unfortunately, the time was not right for us.

IN CONCLUSION

As I was putting this together I was surprised at how bold a traveler I'd become. I'd forgotten about many of those events that kind of scare me today, sitting comfortably on my deck in Americus. I do believe that the good Lord sent angels to watch over me. What a blessing.

For its part The Fuller Center has grown and prospered, probably not as much as it would have had Millard not left us, but I figure he's looking down with a smile on his face as he watches us work to keep his dream alive. Thousands of families across the country and around the world now have a decent place to call home, and it's all due to the loyal donors and volunteers who continue to share so generously of their time and resources. Thank you for being a part of this great movement.

90248539R00080

Made in the USA
Middletown, DE
21 September 2018